PRAISE FOR DEBBIE ROBINS'S
Where Peace Lives

"Peace is generated from consciousness, one person at a time. *Where Peace Lives* is a beautiful invitation to people of every age to engage in the pursuit of peace."

—DEEPAK CHOPRA

"The story is touching, the artwork is beautiful, and the message of peace is so timely. I think the story is destined to become a classic and an inspiration for so many."

—MARIA SHRIVER

"I was charmed."—GORE VIDAL

"In this book, children and adults can find inspiration and get to the source of what really matters in their own lives. It is a roadmap to the soul."

—ARIANNA HUFFINGTON

"When I finished *Where Peace Lives* I felt the same way I did after putting down *The Little Prince*; grateful for the magic of a fable to delight, inspire and educate, all at the same time."

—JANE SEYMOUR

SHOVEL IT!

Kick-Ass Advice

to Turn Life's CRAP into

the Peace and Happiness You Deserve

Debbie Robins

ALYSON*books*

Shovel It:
Kick-Ass Advice to Turn Life's Crap into the Peace and Happiness You Deserve

Copyright © 2009 Debbie Robins

Published by Alyson Books
245 West 17th Street, Suite 1200, New York, NY 10011
www.alyson.com

First Alyson Books edition: January 2010

Library of Congress Cataloging-in-Publication data are on file.

ISBN-10: 1-59350-120-X
ISBN-13: 978-1-59350-120-4

10 9 8 7 6 5 4 3 2 1

Cover design by Lorie Pagnozzi
Book interior by Pauline Neuwirth, Neuwirth & Associates, Inc.

Printed in the United States of America
Distributed by Consortium Book Sales and Distribution
Distribution in the United Kingdom by Turnaround Publisher Services Ltd

ACKNOWLEDGMENTS

*T*O MY HUSBAND, ONE of the most courageous crap-shovelers I know. Thank you for your unending devotion to me. Your insistence I go for my dreams has changed the trajectory of my life.

Heartfelt thanks to all the reactive, depressed, mean, lousy, lying, neurotic, crazy, manic, and angry people I have met. I have compassionately used your pain, and inability to resolve your issues, to teach myself how to create more peace and happiness. Without you I would be less stable and more anxious, less joyful and more depressed, less forgiving and more punitive, less kind and more thoughtless, less optimistic and more cynical, less courageous and unconvinced I can make this adventure however I want it to be.

Thank you to my incredible literary agent, Jason Allen Ashlock, and to my publisher extraordinaire, Don Weise, and everyone at Alyson Books/Here Inc.

Thank you to Pamela Lane, aka The Book Doctor; Lee Cohen, a much better writer than I'll ever be and my dear friend; Drs. Mary and Ron Hulnick, two of the most brilliant psychologists and educators I know. To my friends and family on both sides of the ocean, I love you/ je t'aime! Finally, thanks to my spiritual teacher of thirty-two years, John-Roger, who always has me in his loving arms, and to my Bernese Mountain Dog, whose poop I have learned to lovingly shovel at least once a day.

CRAP-SHOVELING
CONTENTS

SHOVEL IT!

INTRODUCTION: B.Y.O.S.
(BRING YOUR OWN SHOVEL)

Cheer up! The worst is yet to come.

—Anonymous

*L*ET'S FACE IT: there's an enormous amount of crap on this planet and it has to be dealt with. Buddhism teaches that to be human is to suffer, but I think that to be human is to shovel. We're a species bound to shovel life's challenges twenty-four seven. So let's get going!

Thank God we are learning a lot about making intelligent environmental choices. Learning about how to make better decisions in the cars we drive, the lightbulbs we use, and the way we treat our trash. Because that's only half of the problem we have with crap.

The stresses you see in the earth's ecosystems are a lot like what resides in each of our personal ecologies. Whether it's self-generated or inflicted upon you, the pollution of negative thinking, the gas-guzzling appetite of greed, the unregulated dumping of guilt, the noxious fumes of judgment, the destruction of your personal ozone layer from shame, the irresponsible disposal of anger, the disinformation campaign of righteousness—our mental, emotional, and spiritual emissions—choke off your happiness and erode your birthright to live a balanced, peaceful, happy life.

Have you considered the effects of global warming in your brain every time some bozo cuts you off on the freeway, parking lot, or grocery store line? Or your toxicity levels when an automated call system disconnects you after being on hold for twenty-two minutes trying to give a credit card company your change of address so you won't miss a billing cycle and end up in collections? Okay, how about when I mention these two words: *subprime mortgage*. Seeing red or green? What's a good person, wanting to live a more positive, caring, conscious life, to do in a world filled with so many hardships?

If you'd like some answers, then this book is for you. Together, we will courageously face the fact that your well-being is going to be perpetually tested by both conceivable and inconceivable problems. The only recourse is to learn how to survive the onslaught and emerge the victor. Your inner ecology is your responsibility. Just as you are (hopefully!) contributing to the betterment of our global ecological destiny, you must take control of your inner life too.

One good thing about crap is that it's also fertilizer for growth. Used correctly, it is rich in nutrients.

Shortly, I will share with you my seven tried-and-true ways to stay sane on this planet and live a more mentally, emotionally, and spiritually responsible (and just friggin' better) life. I call these techniques my "crap shovelers." I invite you to add them to your coping repertoire if you have one, or use them as a jumping-off place to build your own earth-friendly survival kit.

When you embrace these strategies, use them, and repeat them often enough, you will see phenomenal results. These tools, and others yet to come (Hey, I'm a movie producer: I'm trained to think "sequel"!), will add a vital degree to your educational process: a M.C.S., a Masters in Crap-Shoveling. You can utilize your M.C.S. to keep yourself happy instead of sad, accepting rather than angry, and making choices you will be proud of in the morning instead of ones that will increase your pain after the initial elation of pepper-spraying someone with four-letter words has worn off. All you need is a shovel. A good sense of humor. And the commitment to dig!

1

CRAP-SHOVELING OVERVIEW

A Yogi goes into a pizza parlor and orders a slice with everything on it. He gives the proprietor a $20 bill. The proprietor pockets the money. The Yogi says, "Don't I get change?" The proprietor replies, "Change must come from within.
—Inspired by a joke found on Richard Pettinger's website

*H*ERE'S MY DEFINITION OF mental, emotional, and spiritual crap that can pile up in the corners, crevices, and intersections of your life:

Mental crap: Beliefs that separate you from your commonality and make you want to kick the living daylights out of someone and/or dump all over yourself.

Emotional crap: All hurts, pains, and wounds that cause you to act in ways that harmfully affect yourself and/or others.

Spiritual crap: All uses of God, divine energy, or universal teachings that make you right and the other person wrong, so that the wrong person's life is diminished in value.

According to the Carter Center (as in Jimmy) we live in the most violent (AKA physically, mentally, emotionally, and spiritually crapped up) chapter of human history. Good, decent, kind, ethical, hard-working people are an endangered species. The rich have never been richer, nor the poor poorer. Vast economic disparities have produced deprivation, despair, and a profound sense of disconnection. When people are desperate—which means they no longer have hope—they can act badly. Very badly. Scared people spew emotional smog at the drop of a shovel, forgetting to practice beliefs and philosophies that would reduce harmful exhaust. Much like waiting to see if polar bears can sprout water wings before they all drown, we tend to fantasize about an external solution to our internal debris. We want to be taken over and bailed out like the government did for Fannie Mae, Freddie Mac, AIG, Bank of America, CitiGroup, GM, Chrysler, and the list goes on . . . and on. We dream that success will alleviate our troubles. But it won't. It never has. Hard-earned success is often intersected by tragedy. Just ask Hugh McCutchen, the phenomenal American volleyball coach at the Beijing Olympics whose father-in-law was murdered and who within a week's time won a gold medal.

What then can give us more control over the quality of our lives? One thing for sure: a shovel and your crap-shoveling techniques! They will help you turn your troubles into the peace and happiness you deserve. With them you can build and board the biofueled bus to your own mental, emotional, and spiritual salvation. You will learn to outsmart the down times and have more joy. Recycle your anger and create more sustainable peace. Heal your wounds and enjoy more choice. Learn from others so you don't have to live through every horrible situation yourself. Gain dominion over your mind, emotions, and spiritual beliefs so they are adding value to your human footprint, not raising the disappointment level.

Along the way, become a precycler; that's someone who is conscious about what they buy and chooses products based on waste reduction. Learn to spot the bumps and smooth them out before you bring them home. Become a master crap shoveler and pass your knowledge forward.

2

MY CRAP-SHOVELING STORY

Always remember that you're unique. Just like everyone else.

—A Zen-ism

*I*KNOW YOU'RE PROBABLY anxious to find out, "What's in this book for me?" and I promise, that part is right around the corner, just to the left of your green recycling bin. Let's do a bit of bonding first, and you'll enjoy the "ahas" even more. After all, bonding is our societal code for feeling one another's pain and admitting that no one's life is easy. Getting to know one another may even diminish the sense of aloneness. Here's a bit of my crap-shoveling story.

I always thought of myself as a good candidate for happiness. I was raised with the benefits of an only child because my half sister was fourteen years older and vacated the house when I was born. Was it something I said?

My parents fought like cats and dogs for thirty-five years but never divorced, so I thought I had dodged the bullet of a "broken home." I was well educated and easily got my first job right out of college. That same year, I met my spiritual teacher and began practicing the beliefs found in all great teachings: acceptance, love, and forgiveness. I put those values to good use for twenty years as a film and television producer/executive—ostensibly making movies, but really studying the psychology of seriously out-of-balance people 24/7.

Despite my unyielding work ethic and focus on my spiritual practice, my life was anything but happy. People did horrible things to me and the world at large was a horrible place (from the Cold War to the onslaught of AIDS to the genocide in Bosnia and now Darfur), and I often felt horrible about myself.

My belief that I could find Nirvana, which I defined as perpetual, protracted peace, coupled with my hope that good things were supposed to happen to good people, wasn't panning out. This really pissed me off.

I left my spiritual teacher for four long years, ate too much, drank too much, and spent too much money. I railed against the inequities, ironies, and inconsistencies of my existence in any way I could until, finally, I accepted the ultimate truth: life is a classroom with lesson plans, homework, nice teachers, mean teachers, good grades, bad grades, pop quizzes, gross lunchroom food, unflushed toilets, and graduation day is death. If they make you wear those hideous caps and gowns in heaven, flunk me now. You can choose to be a good student or a jerk-off, a bully or a best friend, a Good Samaritan or a gangbanger.

Even my road-less-traveled-by suffering has been hard. Here's a list, in no particular order, of some of the caca I've lived through.

I have:

- Navigated a childhood where both my parents were manic-depressives (so much for the illusion of stability).
- Divorced because my mother's prophecy on my wedding day came true ("Darling, he's so boring!").
- Parted ways with a family member over a last will and testament that cut her slice of the inheritance pie.
- Had my tonsils out, a hysterectomy, and one cancer scare.
- Had my ears surgically "pinned back" when I was seven because they stuck out and kids teased me relentlessly.
- Moved houses thirteen times in sixteen years (that's a story for another day).
- Suffered through being a stepmom—a no-mom's-land which thankfully is heaven now.
- Experienced my life being turned upside down by someone addicted to heroin. The lying is the hardest part.

- Worked with a narcissistic, downright mean movie director who can't get a film made anymore (gracias, laws of karma).
- Produced a movie that tanked.
- Watched cigarettes suck the life out of both my parents.
- Got fired, struggled to find work, and worked doing things I hated to do.
- Endured rejection by men I thought I was in love with.
- Survived thousands of "no"s as an entertainment producer (movie scripts, television shows, Internet ideas) including 120 literary agents who refused to represent my first book. It ended up on two best-seller lists.
- Gained weight and made promises to lose the weight, which I rarely fulfilled.
- Experienced anti-Semitism from a boyfriend.
- Got robbed in LA of all my jewelry, including pieces my grandmother had given me that her grand-mother had given her.
- Went into menopause at an early age and thought I was losing my mind.
- Lost seventy dollars to a con artist in New York pretending to be the son of Barbara Streisand and Elliott Gould. Babs, where were you when I needed you?

When one problem resolved, the next would arrive—sometimes they even overlapped. I don't know about you, but this was not what I had signed up for in my mother's fallopian tube. (No wonder the first thing a baby does is wail like a motherf——!)

One of the most terrifying times occurred in my midforties. I realized I hated what I was doing and that, after twenty years of working day and night to become a successful entertainment provider, my work had little to no meaning for me. There wasn't a person on my daily hundred-call log sheet I really wanted to talk to. My unhappinessometer was at an all-time high.

I had two choices: change careers or go on antidepressants. I opted for the former because of all the bad crap-shoveling luck, serotonin, which is the primary component found in mood enhancers, makes me feel even more depressed.

Was changing professions painful? Damn right. Was it worth it? Yes. I got coached by Nicholas Lore, one of the pioneers of career coaching, obtained a masters degree in spiritual psychology at the University of Santa Monica in Los Angeles, and began a consulting practice in which I work with clients to help them produce more peace, happiness, and success daily.

I became to others the person I needed in my own moment of crisis—funny how it often works that way. Did finding a purpose-driven life stop bad things from happening? Not a chance, although it did make resolving the mess more worthwhile.

I know that lots of you have had it (and have it) worse. It doesn't matter: it's all crap. And it must be shoveled, survived, and overcome. Mad as hell and unwilling to take it anymore, I decided to fight back.

I dedicated myself to becoming a master crap shoveler. I decided to take back the peace and happiness that is, in my opinion, our divine right. To that goal, I offer you my seven tried-and-true techniques to shovel the crap when it starts to pile up. These techniques will (you can hold me to it):

- Ease your pain (and your anger too).
- Save you from enormous and unnecessary heartache (and doing things you'd regret later, trust me).
- Give you more control over your life despite its insistence on kicking the bejeezus out of you every chance it gets.

So—if you're ready to handle your list, outmaneuver life's suffering, and create more good times when life deals you a "this blows the big one" hand . . . read on. Don't forget to bring one oversized metal shovel, a pair of bright yellow plastic gloves, and a supersized can of lavender air freshener. Target has a great selection. So does L'Occitane. Bien sûr.

3

"SHOULD" IS LIKE A SUBPRIME LOAN; IT'S A SETUP TO BANKRUPT YOU.

Grant me the serenity to accept the things I cannot change, the courage to change the things I can, and the wisdom to hide the bodies of the people I had to kill because they annoyed me.

—Anonymous

OW MANY TIMES a day do you hear yourself, or someone else, say something or someone "should" be different than it is? You're right. A lot.

"Should" is one of the most common auxiliary verbs in our language. Now that you are becoming a master crap shoveler, when "should" creeps into your life, flag the play. The mindset of "should" will only make you feel awful. "Should" suggests there is a right and a wrong, a good and a bad, a "my way or the highway," and that everybody understands the rules and agrees to play by them. But not everybody does.

"Should" is the preamble for cruelly judging oneself. ("I *should* have done that better—am I a loser or what?!"; "I *should* be nicer to that unhappy person because that's what good people do"; "I *should* be more on top of my life and not such a disorganized, distracted mess.") "Should" is also the preamble for cruelly judging others. ("He *should* have done it my way and now everything is messed up"; "She *should* have listened to me rather than being so stubborn"; "They *should* have known better and now we're all going to pay the price.")

Unfortunately, you can't win the "should" game. It's a never-ending loop of assigning blame that easily grows into hatred. And the only one getting hurt by your upset is you. Hatred (of self and others) consumes your thoughts, emotions, and spiritual energy faster than a raging Yosemite fire. It creates a greenhouse effect, trapping pessimism inside you. It is certain to leave you in a smoldering, putrid pile of ashes that might look like fatigue or unprovoked fights or sudden illness.

I am presently dealing with hives that attack my body every night at 3 A.M. Agghhhh . . . time to investigate what I think "should" be different in my life. You will know you're heading toward possible self-destruction the minute you're thinking, *I should be, do, think, feel or behave differently* (referenced above). Or: I'm right + you're wrong = you "should" suffer for your point of view in the most heinous way I can imagine—hee, hee, hee.

The justification for taking your shovel and shoving it in someone's face causes wars, breaks up families, and eliminates the possibility of treating one another as a connected, caring, global mass. Any reason you have for withholding love, dignity, and respect from another living organism engenders more suffering on a planet mired with pain.

Can selfish people (and we are all preoccupied by ourselves) ever commit to put the well-being of others first? I mean really first. Long odds, that's for sure, but you must develop that ability with every unselfish breath you take. Can you nourish your self-esteem so your thoughts, emotions, and spirit will become consistently positive? Better odds here, if you really commit to do the work.

Here are the three "should" statements that used to upset my life and deplete my stockpile of peace and happiness. Perhaps they will stimulate you to identify, analyze, and eradicate yours.

- "I *should* be more successful."
- "He *shouldn't* be fooling around on his wife; it lacks integrity."
- "Everyone *should* be making a difference on this planet instead of focusing on his or her own sorry, spoiled, selfish life."

For example, when I think I "should" be getting more of what I want out of life (given my intelligence, focus, and work ethic), guess what I feel? Angry, despondent, and down (my version of ADD).

When I think one of my best male friends "shouldn't" be having an affair and that if he wants out of his marriage he "should" act with more integrity, guess what I want to do about our long-standing friendship? Throw it down the proverbial drain.

When I think people "should" feel a social responsibility to make our world a better place, imagine what goes on inside me. I loathe my neighbors and dream of having dog poop delivered to their doorsteps. There's actually a company that does this, which tells you a lot about the availability of ordure on this planet. That's the fanciest word for shit I know.

Often times "should" results from an expectation the world owes you justice. I wish. It doesn't. You're screwed.

You've got to figure out an alternative. Much like fossil fuel destroys the planet and clean, renewable energy could save it; you need to ditch the ozone-depleting traditional thinking of "should" and replace it with something better.

I learned this lesson during one of the most frustrating seasons of my life. It encouraged me to convert my "shoulds" back into the inner calm I craved.

I had been wooed for months by a Hollywood movie studio to become part of their newly formed creative team. This is a company whose public promise is to treat their employees like family. I worked my tushy off, arriving at 7A.M., leaving at 8:30 P.M., reading script after script every weekend.

One morning, five months into my two-year contract, I awakened to find a big lump on my back. I had no idea how it got there or how long it had made my spine its home. I was single at the time—relationships were impossible given the workload—so there was no one to observe my body but me.

On my lunch break, I went to my doctor. This meant canceling a meeting with one of the studio's most important directors—not good. My doctor determined the lump must come off immediately. I told my boss and asked for an unheard-of two days off.

When I returned to work with thirteen stitches in my back, grateful for a pathology report pronouncing the lump benign, there was a voice mail inviting me to my boss's office at six o'clock. Our meeting lasted four minutes during which time he suggested we alter my executive stripes to a producing deal. That's Hollywood lingo for "you're fired." The cause: I was no longer the right "fit" for the company. Shocked and in physical pain, I couldn't muster the strength to demand what a "good fit" would look like. Biting my cheek lining, and unsuccessfully trying to stop my tears, I stumbled back into my office.

Sitting on my soon-to-be ex-couch was one of my colleagues. She made me swear on the script for *Casablanca* that our talk would be in confidence. It seems the real reason I was let go was that another executive, a guy the studio had been desperate to hire before me, had suddenly become available.

When my boss asked for more money to bring him in, he was told to let someone go instead. That someone was me.

Here's how I chose to resolve this situation, by using one of the best techniques I know. I call it the **Freedom from "Should" exercise**, also known as the freedom from wanting to kill the cretin for dumping rubbish all over your life. It's a great way to conserve your energy and protect yourself from waste and destruction. It's a solar-powered crap-shoveling technique, and here's how it works.

CRAP-SHOVELING TECHNIQUE #1:

Freedom from "Should"

Write down what pissed you off.

I got fired for no good reason during a very vulnerable time in my life.

What was wrong with what happened?
What would have been right?

What was wrong with what happened is that my boss lied to me. His lies hurt me and made me feel horrible about myself. What would have been right? For him to stand by me and not hire someone else—to demonstrate some integrity, God forbid.

How did this make you feel?

Angry. So furious I wanted to strike out and expose the company as the sick, selfish, dysfunctional place it really is. Spray-painted curse words on the gates to the studio might be a fun place to start.

Take a moment to experience the energy in your body. What's going on?

Sick to my stomach. Heat waves of hurt pulse through my body. If I were a nuclear weapon, you could kiss the planet good-bye.

Take three deep breaths and allow that energy to release. Envision you are a dragon allowing your fire to drain. If it takes more than three, that's okay too.

Breathe. Breathe. Breathe. Okay. Done. It wasn't easy. Maybe I'll take three more breaths to CYA—that's corporate speak for "cover your ass."

Now ask yourself, is there another way to see this situation that would make you feel more positive about it? Share/write that new vision/perspective/point of view.

After being a freelance film/TV producer for so many years, I had been worried about taking an executive job, fearing it would leave me creatively unfulfilled.

In fact, it did. Instead of investing years of my life as an efficient but unhappy "foot soldier," I got out of a bad decision in just months. I also learned a lot about how studios analyze what movies to make, which will help me get my future film projects financed. Hike that up your flagpole, Mr. President of a Studio.

What might you do differently now that you see it this way?
I won't respond with anger. I'll delete the e-mail telling him where to shovel it. I'll stop taking it personally and declare a cease-fire on hating him and judging myself.

Instead, I'm going to pick myself up, dust myself off, and get the movie I'm passionate about done. Success is the best revenge (which is exactly what happened). So is burning garbage to create steam and generate electricity.

On a scale from one to ten (one is no peace, ten is total peace), how do you feel now?
Seven, and that's pushing it, but it sure feels better than level one that had me fantasizing about hiring mafia hit men. Must be watching A&E's *Notorious* series too much.

Now it's your turn. Get out your shovel (and a pad of paper you can use for all the techniques) and start to dig!

Freedom from "Should"

- Write down what pissed you off.
- How did this make you feel?
- Take a moment to experience the energy in your body. What's going on?
- Take three deep breaths and allow that energy to release. Envision you are a dragon allowing your fire to drain. If it takes more, that's okay too.
- Now ask yourself, is there another way to see this situation that would make you feel more positive about it? Share/write that new vision/perspective/point of view.
- What might you do differently now that you see it this way?
- On a scale from one to ten (one is no peace, ten is total peace), how do you feel now?

If, after doing this technique, you experience difficulty in expressing your feelings, or letting go of your sense of unfairness, that's okay. There are deep sentiments and perception shifts I have struggled with too. Building your crap-shoveling muscle takes time. If you want more peace and happiness, patiently learn to stop "shoulding" all over yourself. I am holding that vision for you!

4

I'LL HONK MY HORN
IF I WANT TO, MORON

Suffering is just the other side of happiness.

—*Shantaram* by Gregory David Roberts
(one of my all time favorite books!)

WHY DOES THE world say it wants peace but actually creates less of it? That stinks.

Face it, peace takes time and energy (so does choosing green)—it's hard work and we can all be lazy. "Me" outranks "others" any day of the week.

To avoid the guilt that comes with self-centeredness, we have done a really smart thing. We have made peace an ideal, something we dream about, wish for, and pray to the heavens to deliver more of, to avoid having to exert any effort to make it happen.

On the "I'm trying to outsmart the universe so I really won't have to do the work" spectrum, this thinking surpasses denial, which we groveled in for decades, passively watching violence on the planet escalate and our environment being destroyed.

Unfortunately, peace is not an ideal. Sorry, crap shovelers. Neither is living in a balanced ecosystem. Choosing peace and choosing green are choices. I don't know about you, but my life is jam-packed, without a minute to spare, and if I did have a free second I'd rather answer another e-mail than practice conflict resolution or read about composting. Even getting myself to change detergents to a more earth-friendly brand took months.

The first **"what if" technique** is to quickly exchange your daily disturbances for more harmony while you continue to study, learn, and practice peace in more substantive ways. The second **"what if" technique** encourages you to make more ecological choices. Here's how to do them.

Part One:

I'm driving on Sunset Boulevard in Los Angeles. I like to drive carefully and under the speed limit. Call me crazy. A man in a black Porsche (most fancy cars driven by men in LA are black— a Darth Vader thing) zooms up behind me.

I look in my rearview mirror and he's obviously on his hands-free cell phone, having quite an animated phone conversation, one hand on the wheel, the other gesturing boldly. I accelerate a little to help him feel we're getting wherever he wants to go faster, but this is clearly not good enough for him. He pulls up beside me, revs his engine, and cuts in front of me. A woman now in front of both of us, with two kids in the back of her white gas -guzzling SUV, apparently gets scared by the sound of his engine and brakes. So does he. So do I. We come inches away from multiple fender benders.

Instinctively, three things happen: my right hand reaches for my horn, my left hand quickly rolls down my window, and my mouth prepares to let him know exactly how I feel.

*Remembering that peace is a choice, at every age and in every circumstance, I take a breath and use my **"what if"** technique.*

CRAP-SHOVELING TECNIQUE #2:

The "What If" Technique

- What if he's on the phone with his mother?
- What if his mother's name is Sylvia, like mine?
- What if his mother has just told him his father is in the hospital and that the medications he's received for his heart problems have caused renal failure?
- What if his bold gestures are his upset, fear, and anger toward the ineptitude of the doctors treating his father?

- What if his father is the same age as my father, who is also sick?
- What if the reason he pulls ahead of me is that he's desperate to get to his father's bedside before he dies?

Poor guy. Drive on. Go with speed.

Does it matter if my story is true? No. In fact, I'm sure it's not. He probably is a total piece of work who deserves to be hung upside down by his Dockers. What matters is that the "what if" technique helped me get back to my peace and not add more rage to the road that day. It will help you too.

Remember, use everything to your advantage, including your unique human ability to tell stories to survive the annoyances, inequities, and poor decisions that may affect you.

Part Two:

To begin the "what if" I could be more green technique, make a list of all the things you presently do to help the environment. Here are mine:

- I buy Seventh Generation products (one of the leaders in the environmental movement), including plastic garbage bags, dish detergent, soap, paper napkins, paper towels, and glass cleaner.

- I recycle like a maniac, to the point of checking our nonrecycling can for anything that may have slipped through the cracks, like my husband's Hershey chocolate bar wrappers.
- I drive a MINI Cooper car.
- I talk to our plants, trees, and fauna—telling them I love and respect them.
- I pick up my dogs' poop.
- I even pick up other people's dogs' poop.
- I shop at Whole Foods and other organic markets to buy tomatoes, apples, and lettuces that are organically grown.
- I buy eggs, meat, and poultry only from distributors that treat animals with dignity.

With your list in hand, you can do the "what if I could be more green" technique.

I could:

- Go through every cleaning product I have and find a greener alternative.
- Carpool more with my business partner.
- Learn how to compost trash.
- Read Thomas Friedman's new book about global/green trends. (He rocks my world!)

- Cease and desist from buying plastic water bottles. (This is harder than quitting smoking!)
- Buy a water filtration system.
- Find a flea/tick spray for our dog that isn't toxic but still does the job.
- Learn more about which plants are drought resistant and need less water.
- Make my annual contribution to Healthy Child Healthy World, a phenomenal nonprofit. (Their monthly newsletter is filled with great tips.)

I pass the shovel to you!

SUMMARY

the "what if" technique, part one

- Write down what happened that disturbed your peace.
- Now, make up a story that helps you see the situation or person's actions in a more positive way. What if:

The "what if" technique to be more green, part two:

- Make a list of all the "green" things you presently do.
- "What if" you could be more "green"? What would you do?

The best thing about the "what if" technique is that it's fun to play. You can do it with your family, friends, and coworkers. You'll be amazed at the wonderful stories you'll spin and ideas you'll come up with. And, after you've stopped feeling pissed off about people's inconsiderate behavior, you will feel more benevolent, which is a good thing. Very.

5

WHY THE HELL SHOULD I BE GRATEFUL FOR ALL THE CRAP IN MY LIFE?

Evening news is where they begin with "Good evening," and then proceed to tell you why it isn't.

—A joke my Uncle Charlie told me (and whomever told it to him, I credit you!)

Gratitude: *the quality of being thankful to somebody for doing something.*
Gratitude's synonyms are: *thankfulness, appreciation, and gratefulness.*

*B*E HONEST, DON'T YOU have days where you feel really sick and tired of people telling you to be grateful for the challenges in your life?

Be grateful for what you do have and focus on that.
Bugger off.

Be appreciative of the good deeds done in the world.
Nice try! The bad outweighs the good.

Be grateful you're alive.
Compared to what? Hell? Maybe that's where we are and Mapquest got the directions wrong.

I don't think being a spiritual person hinges on your un-equivocal gratitude for having to shovel through life's physical, emotional, mental, and spiritual hurricanes. I don't want to thank the universe for death, loss, and loneliness. My friend just died at fifty-four, at the height of his career, devastating his wife and two kids.

I don't want to be grateful for financial challenges that kept my family moving from one house to the next (the guys at Box Brothers are my posse), not to mention all the people getting the economic life sucked out of them due to greedy banks, greedy mortgage brokers, and greedy oil companies. There is no good in greed.

Nor do I jump for joy at the aches and pains of growing older and having to endure the hormonal agonies of menopause. The list of wonderful, kind, caring people I know struggling with health issues, particularly cancer, is very long, and if I could,

I'd climb on an angel's wing, zoom up to heaven, and kick whomever is responsible.

So what is all this gratitude crap?

Did you know that shit (and its related emissions) generates a greenhouse gas that destroys our atmosphere? That the cows we raise for meat and milk create more global warming than trains, planes, and cars? Well, think of gratitude as a powerful way to keep the turmoil in our lives from overwhelming our personal ecosystem in destructive ways. Gratitude is the equivalent of holding a match up to a cow's ass and lighting his or her fart before it gets to the ozone layer.

An honest reason to choose gratitude is a selfish one. Gratitude makes you feel better. Gratitude brings you happiness while lack of gratitude makes you feel bad. Personally, I detest feeling down. Let's see . . . more happiness . . . or more depression/anxiety/misery. A no-brainer. Gratitude, like it or not, is the quickest route I know to help you feel better when life deals you a tough blow. Let's sign up for gratitude class. We'll sit in front and share the serenity.

When you find yourself wanting to rail against the pain, suffering, and sheer thoughtlessness that exists, engage yourself in my gratitude technique. Start by identifying what's bothering you, the situation that's got your dander up. Let's say I'm upset because I submit a screenplay to an old friend, a well-known producer, anticipating he will enjoy it and want to get involved. Instead, he calls me on the phone and rips the script apart, scene by scene. There is virtually nothing he likes, not its premise, its characters, or its commercial viability. The way in which he delivers the assessment isn't soft, warm, or fuzzy. I put down the phone convinced I'll never work in Hollywood again. I'm not experiencing any gratitude for this moment in my life. Not one bit.

CRAP-SHOVELING TECHNIQUE #3:

"The vodka tonic's half full and I'm grateful for my olive" technique

Spell gratitude with me—because, crap shovelers, it's time to boogie with the God of thankfulness!

GIMME A G: What's the one thing that's *good* about this situation?

I've just lived through one of my worst nightmares. I feel like nothing anyone else could say would ever hurt like this again. (Was I mistaken!) I'm grateful to my friend, who I'll never, ever, speak to again, for opening his big, unkind mouth. Twisted logic? Maybe. Sometimes the greatest blessing is to get the worst over so it's downhill after that.

GIMME AN R: What's the *recurring* feeling or emotion this situation brings up that you struggle with in other areas of your life?

Feeling a loss of control, an inability to make my dreams come true. I never thought it would take this long. Aagghhhh . . . impatience has reared its ugly head again. I hate my life. I never get a break. These thoughts are certain to cause me to give up.

GIMME AN A: What's your *accountability* to this situation? What part did you play in creating it?

I haven't seen my friend in a long time and rather than have lunch with him first, to get a sense of the kind of material he's looking for, I e-mailed the script to him. I tend to act impulsively, because I want immediate results, and it can cause me unnecessary pain.

Perhaps now I'll learn the lesson and change my ways— use it as an opportunity to break out of an old, destructive pattern. To quote John Wayne: "I'm gonna check you out real good, before I let you take my pistol again." (I actually made this up, sorry. John Wayne never said this, but he could have.)

GIMME A T: What *turns* this situation around?

Reminding myself that, despite the thousands of "no"s I've heard, I have been involved in the making of seven movies, launched a successful consulting company, and published two books.

I'm grateful that, at my core, I'm strong like a bull, which doesn't mean I don't get hurt. I do. Seeking success can suck a lot of joy out of you. Believing you can make a difference keeps you going. Besides, what else are you going to do while you're stuck on this totally screwed-up, magnificently beautiful planet?

GIMME AN I: What *ideally* do you want to happen?

I want to find producers/financiers who love the film as much as I do and will get it made.

I'm grateful I've watched the Academy Awards my whole life, and heard the same story again and again: "It took ten years but finally someone believed in me."

[Beware of trashing my script. One billion people watch the Oscars and I might decide not to thank my mother and father and tell the world about how you rejected me instead.]

GIMME A T: What further *turns* this situation around?

Creating a list (My name is Deb and I'm a "list-aholic") of more people I can show the script to—with a reminder to quiz them on their likes and dislikes before sending it to them.

I'm happy there are a lot of wannabes who want to be in the movie business. It's an endless source of possibilities. More painful times ahead? Sure. Why do it? Why not? I've got to do something creative. It's in my DNA. Might as well do this.

GIMME A U: What *underlying* negative belief do you have that is co-creating this situation?

I've deluded myself into thinking I have talent as a writer. I don't. I came to writing late in my life and it shows.

Nice thinking, Robins. That'll get you where you want to be. I appreciate seeing how my belief might be creating my unsatisfying reality. If I could resurrect the philosopher Descartes—you know, the guy who said, "I think, therefore I am"—I'd whack him upside his head with my favorite shovel before cleaning it off. Don't you just hate how powerful the mind is?! Unless, of course, you learn to use it for your advancement.

GIMME A D: What might you *dare* to do differently to create a better outcome for yourself?

I'll recommit to doing whatever it takes to get the movie made, regardless of the rejections I might have to endure.

Did you know the mind doesn't know the difference between fantasy and reality? I'll act as if every "no" brings me closer to my "yes," which mathematically it does. Too bad emotions aren't as predictable as numbers.

GIMME AN E: What positive *end* result can you envision as a product of this situation?

Someday and somehow, a powerful producer, star or financier will love my script and want to make it, and my perseverance pays off. I've never felt more jazzed. Rejection can actually be energizing. I can't wait to run into my friend and share my good news!

It's your chance. Say "gratitude" ten times fast and get going!

"The vodka tonic's half full and I'm grateful for my olive" technique

- Describe the *incident* that upset you.
- **GIMME A G:** What's the one thing that's *good* about this situation?
- **GIMME AN R:** What's the *recurring* feeling or emotion this situation brings up that you struggle with in other areas of your life?
- **GIMME AN A:** What's your *accountability* to this situation? What part did you play in creating it?
- **GIMME A T:** What *turns* this situation around?
- **GIMME AN I:** What *ideally* do you want to happen?
- **GIMME A T:** What further *turns* this situation around?
- **GIMME A U:** What *underlying* negative belief do you have that is co-creating this situation?
- **GIMME A D:** What might you *dare* to do differently to create a better outcome for yourself?

- **GIMME AN E:** What positive *end* result can you envision as a product of this situation?

You have no control over what goes on out there. But you do have total control over what goes on inside yourself, what you do about your disturbance. Using this technique will increase your ability to find the good in everything that happens. Try it. I really think you'll like it. Perhaps you'll even feel grateful you have it in your bag of crap-shoveling tricks.

6

SHOW ME THE MONEY!

Son: "Daddy, I have to write a special report for school, but I don't know what Politics is."

Father: "Well, let's take our home as an example. I am the breadwinner, so let's call me Capitalism. Your Mum is the administrator of money, so we'll call her Government. We take care of your need, so let's call you the People. We'll call the maid the Working Class, and your brother we can call the Future. Do you understand, son?"

Son: "I'm not really sure, Dad. I'll have to think about it."

That night, awakened by his brother's crying, the boy went to see what was wrong. Discovering that the baby had seriously soiled his diaper, the boy went to his parents' room and found his mother sound asleep. He went to the maid's room, where, peeking through the keyhole, he saw his father in bed with the maid. The boy's knocking went totally unheeded by his father and the maid, so the boy returned to his room and went back to sleep.

The next morning he reported to his father.

Son: "Dad, now I think I understand what Politics is."

Father: "Good, son! Can you explain it to me in your own words?"

Son: "Well, Dad, while Capitalism is screwing the Working Class, Government is sound asleep, the People are being completely ignored, and the Future is full of shit."

—Anonymous story found on the Internet

*M*ONEY ISSUES KEEP therapists thriving. It is the number one problem cited for animosities between friends, business associates, spouses, families, and nations. We blame money for everything. Consider whether you've heard yourself make any of the following statements lately:

- "All my spouse/life partner and I do is fight about money."
- "More money would solve all my problems."
- "Money screws everything up."

Could it be that your present relationship with money does, literally, muck things up? Money is a lot like ozone. Ozone is a delicate chemical that provides a shell around the earth's atmosphere to shield you against deadly radiation that would give you skin cancer and cataracts and damage your immune system. Too little and you get sick, too much and it gets down here, where you breathe, which is not where it belongs. So you need it, that's for sure, but too much going to the wrong places, or too little, really screws it up. The moral: only you can decide how much money you need and whether your emphasis on money is helping you live a happier life.

There's another thing I have come to understand about money. Money acts as a magnifying glass for whatever is going on inside of you. If you're feeling insecure, the acquisition of more wealth will increase your insecurities. If you're feeling anxious, money will heighten your worry. If you feel secure, generous, and great, money will provide opportunities to express that too. The real problem, always, is that your pain seeks out money, thinking money will make it go away. The hurt never does. I can't tell you how many actors, executives, and entrepreneurs I've known who have come into great wealth, only to discover that their problems are the same.

Although I can't name names, I was told by my friend who is a top corporate consultant that one of the richest men in America gets a report showing the number of rolls of toilet paper used at his company on a weekly basis. He's afraid of going broke and there is no amount of money that will squelch his fear. God only knows what happened to him when he was a child.

If you hear yourself blaming your unhappiness on money, it's time to get out your shovel and start digging for the confusion, hurt, indoctrination, and negative beliefs you have surrounding wealth. We all have hangups. Welcome to the human race. Your money issues are your treasure map to finding them. Once you uncover them, do something about it. That way, you will translate your money troubles into an asset that can pay you lifelong dividends.

I'm passionate about good, caring, concerned people creating as much wealth as possible, and I work diligently with my private and corporate clients to ensure that happens. The first place we turn is making sure they have a "purpose" for their lives.

In one of my favorite movies, *Jerry Maguire*, Tom Cruise's character goes from enormous wealth and power—albeit with a life devoid of love, friends, and any form of connection—to not having much bling to show off. It is not until he discovers the value of human connections that his life ramps back up. With his purpose in hand—to impeccably (and ethically) serve his one client—he not only gets the money, he gets Renee Zellweger and the cutest kid on the planet.

If you feel you don't know your purpose, you might want to get out your explorer's hat and answer my **Three Purpose Questions**. They are designed to reveal your future. Then, it is incumbent upon you to invent a vocation (job, career, professional commitment) that allows you to accomplish your true calling.

Remember, if you want to make money and you want to be happy, make your purpose your Federal Reserve; it feeds and funds you.

CRAP-SHOVELING TECHNIQUE #4:

"You had me at 'I'll buy lunch!'"

Purpose question #1:

Imagine you have one billion dollars. That's a bucket full of money! Assume you have taken care of all your needs—clothes, houses, cars, jewelry, vacations, education—and the needs of your family and friends. With all that out of the way, what national or global challenge would you set out to solve? What cause/issue would you get involved with? Where would you like to see your money make a difference? Feel free to do some research if you don't already know.

Mine is education. I would spend my billion dollars on creating better educational institutions and practices for the children of our world.

Purpose question #2:

A genie with a magic lamp has just arrived at your home. After a nice cup of chai, the genie asks you to make three wishes for the planet, things you believe will make the world a better place. What are your three requests?

When the genie visited me (and mine asked for a single decaf espresso), these were my requests:

- I wish for nations/countries to learn how to agree to disagree and act for the common good.

- I wish for an educational revolution that will include the teaching of peace.

- I wish for new societal models to heal the incongruities between rich and poor and utilize our resources to the advantage of all people.

Purpose question #3:

If there was a theme to your work, an overriding philosophy, what would that be? This is not what you do (I'm an acupuncturist, writer, mother, construction supervisor) but rather the reason why you do it that gives your life meaning. Example: a person might choose pediatric medicine because they're passionate about creating strong foundations for young people. Granted, there are other ways to fulfill that mission (mother, teacher, priest) but becoming a pediatrician certainly works. Your purpose is your engine. Your profession is your preference.

The premise of my life's work is helping people create more happiness so they can contribute to greater world peace. Are you at all surprised I became a consultant/coach, helping individuals and companies solve their problems? Or that I authored books like *Where Peace Lives, Where Happiness Lives*, and the one you now hold? Of course you're not. I'm living my purpose, being ecosmart, and making money too.

Let's dream of big shovels in the sky and create your living vision.

SUMMARY

"You had me at 'I'll buy lunch!'"

- *Purpose question #1:* Pretend you have one billion dollars. That's a bucket full of money! Assume you have taken care of all your needs—clothes, houses, cars, jewelry, vacations, education—and the needs of your family and friends. With all that out of the way, what national or global challenge would you set out to solve? What cause/issue would you get involved in? Where would you like to see your money make a difference?

- *Purpose question #2:* A genie with a magic lamp has just arrived at your home. After a nice cup of chai, the genie asks you to make three wishes for the planet, things you believe will make the world a better place. What are your three requests?

■ *Purpose question #3:* If there was a theme to your life, a philosophy, what would that be?

What might someone like you do in the world to fulfill your life's purpose?

Once you know your purpose, everything will make sense, feel whole, and be on track, even if the world seems upside down. You will know what to say yes to, what to say no to, and where to expend your energy. Your purpose defines your choices. Some days, when I take the subway in New York City, I'm convinced we're living in a loony-bin with no hope of ever getting out. Thank goodness you get to keep your shovel and your life focus. Insane asylum or just plain life, be appreciative every day you know why you're here and what you're meant to do. If you don't know, now is the time to find out. No more excuses! Too self-indulgent.

7

ONE MORE AFFIRMATION AND I'LL KILL MYSELF

A disastrous flood came to town. This man had an absolute belief that God always would save him. Flood waters took over his yard. He went on to his front porch. A boat came by.

Boatman: "Come on, I will take you to higher ground."

The man: "Don't bother. God will save me."

The water rose higher and higher. The water was up to his knee, then his waist. So he climbed on to the porch roof. A second boat came by.

Boatman: "Come on, get in. I will take you to higher ground."

The man: "Don't bother. God will save me."

The water rose higher and higher. He climbed to the house roof. Then a helicopter found him.

Helicopter pilot (by public address system): "Grab hold of the rope that we will throw down, to pull you in."

The man: "Don't bother. God will save me."

The water rose higher and higher, until the man drowned. Very angry, he met with St. Peter.

The man: "I was taught that God always will save me. I really am disappointed. Why didn't he save me?"

St. Peter: "If you have any complaint, God is in the next office. You have my permission to go in there and talk to God personally."

So he walked into God's office.

The man: "I really am disappointed. Why didn't you save me?"

God: "Look, I sent you two boats. Then I sent you a helicopter. What more do you want?"

—Lester Hemphill's Internet site of spiritual jokes

*T*HE LAST TEN years may come to be known as the decade of affirmations, a time when intelligent people plastered positive statements everywhere, forgetting how to leave refrigerator doors uncluttered.

These are three of my favorite affirmations:

"I am one with my universe."

How the heck do you pull that off? Board a spaceship to the outer rim of our galaxy where all boundaries cease to exist? Book a therapy session with the Almighty hoping for a major breakthrough in your relationship? Yeah, that's probably it.

"I am seeing the perfection in all things."

What pair of glasses are you wearing?! If I were an eye doctor instead of an author, producer and coach, I'd give you contact lenses dipped in Prozac to manifest that result. There is no perfection on this planet. Get a grip.

"I am open to receive the abundance."

I agree with that one. You can bank on an abundance of more crap coming your way.

Our desire to affirm our dreams has birthed an entire cottage industry of cards, stones, banners, and jewelry. Somebody's getting rich. The question is, has life gotten any easier because you keep saying it is? You decide.

Once, I repeated an affirmation one hundred times: "I am being showered with health, wealth, and prosperity." It felt great in the moment until I went to my mailbox and discovered a doctor's bill for eleven hundred dollars that my medical insurance company was refusing to pay. I never said that affirmation again.

Hallmark affirmations are even worse. They are like the people who brag about recycling to save the planet, then fill their bins full of empty individual-sized plastic water bottles, which are delivered to their door by a huge, carbon-monoxide-spewing truck every week.

Although I have removed all angel cards from my life, there is one technique I still get value from. That's probably because it inflates my ego, which is always looking for a good pat on the back. I call it the **Mirror-Mirror Technique**, and it inverts an ancient school of psychology based on negative projections into something, yes, affirming.

Since the time of Jung and probably earlier, therapists have listened to patients rant and rave about the screwed up people in their lives, and then tried to explain to them that their judgments were really negative projections—a window into their own personality flaws and deep seated issues they had "projected" on to others. Example: if a boss consistently labels his employees as disrespectful, guess what . . . the boss is most likely disrespectful in his/her behavior too.

If a wife wants to leave her husband because he never seems present in their relationship, lo and behold . . . a part of her checked out on the marriage too. If a teenage boy complains that his parents are too hard on him, you nailed it . . . secretly, he is brutal on himself.

At some point, forward-thinking psychologists began to wonder if projections could occur on the positive side of our natures. If you admire and respect someone, is there information embedded in those feelings about your internal wiring too? Yes, there is.

Okay, I really admire Oprah Winfrey. To me, she displays courage, intelligence, humor, caring, philanthropy, inexhaustible energy, and an unstoppable dedication to change the world, one story at a time. If I am self-centered, then what I see in Oprah must be a reflection of qualities that reside in me. Mirror, mirror, who's the most incredible person of them all? Huh, I like that!

Mirror-Mirror Technique

The basic format I am about to show you was taught to me at the University of Santa Monica, in Los Angeles, California, where I earned my master's degree in spiritual psychology.

Name a person, alive or dead, famous or not famous, who you really respect. Write down the qualities you see in them that are so fantastic.

> Oprah Winfrey: courageous, intelligent, funny, caring, philanthropic, energetic, inexhaustible, dedicated to changing the world one story at a time.

Convert their qualities into statements about yourself. Always begin with I am:

> I am courageous.
>
> I am intelligent, humorous, caring, and philanthropic.
>
> I am filled with inexhaustible energy and an unstoppable dedication to change the world one story at a time.

I adore positive projections. And yes, they are also affirmations sourced in a different way, so call me a hypocrite and get it off your chest. They make you feel strong, aligned, and in touch with the best of who you are.

Do you think Oprah gets dissed? You bet she does. No one is exempt from life's lessons. It's just that her shovel is plated in gold, and her personal assistant polishes it twice daily. Am I jealous? Not one bit. She's earned it. Go Oprah.

Your turn! Polish your shovel and enjoy the reflection.

SUMMARY

Mirror-Mirror Technique

- Name a person, alive or dead, famous or not famous, who you really respect.
- Write down the five qualities you see in them that are so fantastic.
- Convert those qualities into statements about yourself. Always begin with "I am."

By remembering to do your positive projections you can pick yourself up whenever you feel down. You don't have to wait for someone to tell you how great you are. You can advocate for yourself. Blow your own horn. Beat your own drum. I'll be standing on the sidelines cheering you on!

8

WHAT SOMEONE FORGOT TO TELL YOU ABOUT THE SECRET

This fellow was climbing a tree when suddenly he slipped. He grabbed a branch and was hanging there. After an hour or so passed, he was feeling exhausted. He looked up to the heavens and cried out: "God, help me, please, help me." Suddenly the clouds parted and a deep voice resounded, "Let go!" The guy paused and looked up at heaven once more, and said: "Is there anyone else up there?"

—Anonymous

WHAT BUGS ME ABOUT the book *The Secret*, an important literary contribution with relevant information, is its refusal to tell the whole truth. You don't always get everything you ask for. Period. I don't know anyone who has everything they want and if you do, have them text me.

While I believe wholeheartedly in vision and the power of

intentions—they are cornerstones of my consulting practice—I also know you have to be at peace with how the cookie crumbles in your life. That's why I always end my prayers with these words: This or Something Better for the Highest Good. I never presume to know what is best for me. I never presume to know timelines. I never presume to know how, when, or in what form something I want will manifest. And if it doesn't manifest, I make that okay too.

It's so hard to trust. It takes an enormous amount of experience, focus, and courage to allow results to happen. I stumble with my trust factor all the time. But when I do, I reach for my shovel and start to dig. You can shovel away your need to control too. It will leave you basking in the glow of a more co-creative process. The decision to take your ego out of the equation (I suggest you read Eckhardt Tolle's brilliant bestseller, *The New Earth*. Boy, that man is smart!) will save you from the agony of unfulfilled expectations. It will also help you find value in what does show up, even if it is different than you envisioned.

For instance, if you visualize buying a fancy sports car and end up making only enough money to purchase a used but perfectly oiled Volvo that saves your life in a head-on accident, I suspect you'd be okay with that. Perhaps, had you been driving the Porsche, you might be dead, and until we have proof heaven's a laugh riot, I suggest you hang on here for as long as you can. At best, the odds are 50/50 you'll get what you want exactly the way you want it, and sometimes the odds are worse than that. You will get results though, and hopefully they'll be just as sweet.

Some researchers in Florida were walking through a lumberyard checking out the toxic waste. They found this fern, called a brake fern, growing in dirt, heavily contaminated with arsenic. And it wasn't just hanging on, it was thriving. Turns out, the plant loves arsenic and soaks it up like crazy, removing it from the soil in the process.

There are other plants, the sunflower for example, that drink up toxins too, like lead in contaminated factory sites and nuclear radiation in Chernobyl. Scientists were searching for ways to clean up the massive amounts of toxic waste we have spilled on this planet—they were intent on finding solutions and they were pleasantly surprised that the answers came out of nature. Good intention. Surprise. Happy ending.

To help yourself create what you want while simultaneously trusting the universe to decide what form it is meant to come in, consider writing what I call a **Living Vision**.

CRAP-SHOVELING TECHNIQUE #6:

"Getting down with the universe" Technique

Start by having a clear picture in your head of the biggest, boldest, most fulfilling life you can imagine living. Think of your life as a designer suit, made just for you (Ralph Lauren is my favorite designer so I just imagine Ralphy baby and me making fashion history together) and when the public sees you, heads turn.

Now, write about who you are and what you're doing in glorious detail. Do not describe how you got there. You are there! Don't forget to use lots of adjectives because they excite our inner child ("I want a car" . . . boring to the inner child. "I want a fast, slick, sexy, safe, cushy Batmobile" . . . now your inner child is interested).

Here is one of my living visions, and remember, *"This or something better for the highest good."*

> *I am a happily published author of global bestsellers that touch the hearts and souls of many. I am a renowned and sought-after coach/consultant working with great individual and corporate clients whose lives are transforming as a result of our time together. I am a successful Hollywood screenwriter and producer, making films that my husband is brilliantly directing. My life is in total flow—it is fun, productive, service oriented, philanthropic, and celebratory. I am experiencing extraordinary health and prosperity. I am filled with gratitude for all that I have. I am living the life of my dreams, being authentically who I am, joyfully learning and growing, enjoying my journey to Shovel It!, consciously turning life's crap into the peace and*

happiness I deserve. This or something better for the highest good.

Get writing, crap shovelers!

"Getting down with the universe" Technique

- Get a clear picture in your head of the biggest, boldest, most fulfilling life you can imagine living.
- Write about who you are and what you're doing in glorious detail. Do not describe how you got there. No. You are there!
- Don't forget to use lots of adjectives because they engage your inner child to get excited.
- Always end a living vision with: *This or something better for the highest good.*

The reason you ask that your vision be for the highest good is that you don't want to mistakenly create circumstances that hurt other people. Imagine if you beg the universe for a big job, with a big pay raise, but you specify you'd like it in New York City (because you think it will be glamorous there) even though you reside in Detroit. You get the position, but now your wife has to quit her job, your kids have to leave their schools, and your dog, who is too old to travel, has to be put down—by the time you get resituated your family has fallen apart. Had you asked, "for the highest good," you might have gotten the better job with better pay in your hometown, saving your loved ones grief.

Lastly, stay open to the possibility that what the universe has in store for you is larger than what you can presently imagine. I once envisioned a cable television series of mine going forward. I prayed for it daily and waited for divine intervention. But the cable channel fell into bankruptcy and my series went down the drain too. En route to my bed, where I intended to stay for the rest of my life, I got a call from a major Hollywood movie director. He wanted me to run his company that was about to produce a movie with Paul Newman. (Yes, his eyes were that blue.) You can guess what my answer was. To this day, I thank my lucky stars I didn't make that cable series. I bet you have an experience like that in your life, where not getting something you wanted opened another door to a superior result. If you do, engrave the memory on your forehead, okay?!

9

I HATE YOU, I HATE YOU, I HATE YOU!

In Jerusalem, an American tourist hears about an old rabbi who visits the Wailing Wall to pray, twice a day, every day, and has been doing so for a long, long time. The tourist watches the rabbi pray, and when he seems to be done, the tourist asks:

"How long have you been coming to the Wailing Wall?"
"For about fifty years," he replies.
"What do you pray for?" the tourist inquires.
"I pray for peace between the Jews and the Arabs. I pray for global warming to be stopped, and I pray for all our children to grow up educated and safe."
"How do you feel it's going after fifty years?"
"Like I'm talking to a f—— wall!"

—My father's favorite story . . .
that he never got tired of telling for fifty years!

I DON'T KNOW IF there are "bad" people in the world (I've yet to gaze at a baby and think, *that's a bad person waiting to happen*) but God only knows, some people grow up, get hurt, and act badly—very badly—and their behavior negatively affects others. Embedded in every culture, nation, and generation are people who kill, rape, torture, and injure others in the name of some higher purpose, usually their own self-interest. There is always wrongdoing on this planet, always. We have not learned how to play nice and, perhaps, never will.

Your day-to-day life may not be as devastating as those who know war firsthand, but it can be harsh nevertheless, and everything is relative. People who lie, cheat, and steal have screwed up my life. I have been hurt by selfish, political, and prejudicial actions. It's hard to read the morning paper, watch the nightly news, or drive from point A to B without being assaulted by someone else's rage. My friend Lauri Burrier calls it "being slimed." I bet you get slimed too.

Yesterday, I waited patiently in my car before turning right, allowing two thirty-something women with two young kids and one blue baby carriage to cross the street. Finally, they started on their way. The one holding the hands of the children said something to one child that caused him to start crying. The two women stopped, abruptly turned around, and yanked both toddlers by the arm back to the corner. Feeling compassion for all involved (parenting isn't easy, nor is growing up), and anticipating they'd be there for a while, I carefully accelerated and began to make my turn. At that exact moment, they decided to cross the street again, forcing me to break. The lady pushing the stroller looked up at me and shouted, "Asshole! There are kids on the street, for Christ's sake!"

I don't care if this woman is having a bad day, bad year, bad life, generated by her bad childhood experiences. I know a lot of people with gruesome beginnings who are nice, human beings. Sometimes compassion is totally overrated. Yesterday was one of those days. I thought of turning my car around, driving up on the sidewalk, jumping out, throwing her up against a wall, and scaring the crap out of her until she apologized. Yeah . . . that's what I wanted to do. Crap-Shoveling Techniques 1–6 just weren't going to cut it.

But I couldn't, and here's why. The biggest problem with embracing vengefulness is how awful it makes you feel. When you engage in hurting others it eats away at you, like acid rain devours our planet. Faster than you can say, "Sit on this and rotate," your energy level drops, you can't focus on your work, and you waste your time telling your version of the story to anyone who will listen, reinforcing why you were right and the other person was wrong. If that's the case, act fast, before you blow a deadline, weaken your immune system or do something you'll regret.

Here's my remedy for justifiable anger that even meditation, back-to-back aerobics classes, and a good bottle of cabernet sauvignon can't quiet:

CRAP-SHOVELING TECHNIQUE #7:

Defcon Nine Technique

Find some paper, at least four sheets (No computers, Iphones or BlackBerries allowed). I like light blue, lined notepads from Staples best. Place your pen or pencil on the paper and begin writing for a minimum of five minutes (fifteen is better) without stopping or allowing your scribing utensil to leave the paper. Write exactly what comes into your mind: every negative, nasty, judgmental, mean, cruel, explicit, hostile, threatening, and reprehensible thought you have. Hold nothing back. No one is exempt since you will NEVER read this diatribe nor will anyone else. It doesn't matter if it makes sense or not, just write.

Here's the beginning part of what mine looked liked after I allowed a miserable woman to ruin my day:

> Crap. Hate you. I can't believe the world lets people like you out of their cage. Red. Heat. Toddlers. Caca poopoo. Pain, rage, want to ram my car right up your . . . people suck. So do Mondays. Gandhi was a fool. So am I. Old soul, tired of the crap. Hate you, hate you, hate you . . . HATE YOU. Hope your kid bites your nipple next time you're breastfeeding.

You get the drift. Keep writing until you have exhausted your negative thoughts. Hold back nothing. Then do one of two things. If at all possible, burn the paper in a safe place like a fireplace. I don't advise ashtrays, lawns, or garbage cans because Murphy's crap-shoveling law will probably result in a fire. If burning your pages is not an option, tear them up into small pieces and throw them away. Flush them and watch them swirl away down the toilet. Do not, under any circumstances, read what you have written. Let it all go, all the disapproving emotions. You will feel more of two things: relaxed and less affected by the walking wounded who step on your toes constantly.

You're up to bat. Let it rip!

SUMMARY

Defcon Nine Technique

- Begin writing down every negative thought you have. Leave no crude metaphor unturned.
- Once you are done, take the sheets of paper and safely burn them or tear them into small pieces and throw them away.
- Remember: never read what you have written or let anyone else read it!

Free-form writing is the most effective way I know to vacuum up your anger. I'm a clean freak, so I love to dispense with dirt. Even if you don't, do this technique at least once a month. Garbage piles up in your consciousness without you even knowing it. Only you are responsible for taking it to the dump.

You now have seven strategies to turn life's crap into the peace and happiness you deserve. Four of them—the What If Technique, Freedom from "Should," Gratitude, and Free-form Writing will stabilize your mind and emotions when life deals you a rotten hand. Mirror-Mirror and Living Vision will fortify your inner spirit so you can sustain the rugged ride with more ease, grace, and belief in your self. I promise you they work. Not a day goes by that I don't reach into my tool kit, grab a skill, and help myself have a good day rather than a troubled one. The beauty of crap-shoveling practices is that they work equally well on big and small challenges. Bottom line: your peace and happiness are precious commodities. Do whatever it takes to protect them.

10

FOURTEEN BELIEFS THAT ARE UTTER CRAP AND HOW TO DIG OUT FROM UNDER THEM

Belief #1:

▶ **MEDITATION STOPS THE MIND FROM THINKING**

Not true! (Unless you're Buddha.) While meditation can absolutely make you feel calmer about the problems in your life, your mind will never totally turn off when you meditate, which I have done almost every day for thirty-two years.

If someone suggests your meditation is a failure if your mind remains active, tell him or her where to shovel their mental capabilities.

You are composed of four distinct psychological quadrants: the physical, the mental, the emotional, and the spiritual. The physical is concerned with bodily functions. The emotions do nothing but feel. The spiritual works to ascend the other three levels, and the mind has only one job—to think. Even when you sleep (theoretically your most "meditative" time) you are thinking, even if it shows up more like an LSD trip. Last night I dreamt I was a male bison, in love with a female buffalo, racing to save her from her overbearing father who wanted her to follow another herd. Perhaps my mind is telling me to get in touch with my animal instincts and live life more boldly; or rather, to have sex with my fabulous husband of twenty years because in a long-term marriage, regardless of deep intimacy, you can forget to nurture the physical sometimes. Or, to work harder to ensure that racism is eradicated in this country and we become one colorblind herd. Only the mind knows for sure and it likes to keep going around the clock.

Here's my suggestion: when you meditate (which I strongly encourage), let your mind do whatever it wants to do. Pay no attention to your thoughts. Don't try to stop them, edit them, or change them. Your thoughts are fine exactly the way they are. If your mind wants to make a list, let it. If it wants to review the same information over and over again, no worries. If you find yourself filled with anxiety, worrying about everything from your scale mistakenly telling you you've gained a pound to nuclear proliferation, no biggie. Keep meditating anyway and pat yourself on the back each time you do.

The commitment to sit your butt down, chant a tone, follow guided imagery, or do whatever else you do as part of your mediation practice is all the universe needs to work its magic.

In my experience, during or after a meditation you can easily source new ideas, find creative solutions to problems, and always be reminded we are not our body, mind or emotions, but something far bigger—like geothermal energy from within the earth. Whether you call it God, divine energy, or universal consciousness, meditation invites that energy in and makes you feel more willing to work with the challenges, even amidst the endless mental chatter.

> A student went to his meditation teacher and said, "My meditation is horrible! I feel so distracted, or my legs ache, or I'm constantly falling asleep. It's just horrible!"
>
> "It will pass," the teacher said matter-of-factly.
>
> A week later, the student came back to his teacher. "My meditation is wonderful! I feel so aware, so peaceful, so alive! It's just wonderful!"
>
> "It will pass," the teacher replied matter-of-factly.
>
> —Anonymous

Belief #2:
▶ **SERVICE IS SELFLESS**

Whoever got this belief going, that service is selfless, should be shot. Service is anything but selfless. Service is totally selfish. We're self-involved. Get used to it. To serve means to do something for someone that has no direct self-serving impact on our life—it doesn't make us wealthier, prettier, thinner, smarter, or more famous. Then why do it? The initial reason, like practicing gratitude, is that it makes you feel good.

Service brings out the best in you and that feels exhilarating. Your own issues take a back seat to those that you are helping and that is liberating. It connects you to your heart and that's the finest dessert on the menu of life . . . sweet, incredibly sweet, and once you've tasted some, you only want more. This is why I insist that each client I work with has some form of giving back embedded in his or her professional design. If they do, they'll be happier. I like being around happy people. I bet you do too.

I don't believe Mother Teresa served the poorest of the poor because she felt she "should" do it. I doubt that Bill and Melinda Gates give their money away because they believe a moral bullet is pointed at their heads. I feel certain Oprah does not do the gazillion great things she does because she's guilty about her success. They have each found a way to give back that lets them know themselves better. Selfishly, that feels hotter than an aphrodisiac and in the process positively impacts the world.

Using Mother Teresa again as an example, she wanted, more than anything, to experience God. In modern lingo, it was her "intention." This is what she wrote:

Help me to spread Thy fragrance everywhere I go. Flood my
soul with Thy spirit and love. Penetrate and possess my whole

being so utterly that all my life may only be a radiance of Thine. Shine through me and be so in me that every soul I come in contact with may feel Thy presence in my soul. Let them look up and see no longer me but only God. Stay with me and then I shall begin to shine as you shine, so to shine as to be a light to others.

It's so easy to understand why she chose to serve the way she did. It brought out the best of who she was and what she wanted. While serving the poor was perfect for Mother Teresa, it might not be perfect for you. Or me. That's a-okay.

There is one additional benefit about service. Apparently, doing good work in the world can improve your health. A Harvard psychologist named David McClelland devoted a large portion of his career to studying the effects of charitable behavior on personal well-being.

After showing a group of college students a film on the life and work of Mother Teresa, McClelland observed that their immune systems grew stronger (determined by tracking a certain protein related to wellness). It seems that even thinking about doing good deeds made them more resilient.

Selfishly, I want to live a long and healthy life. That's why I eat organic chocolate, take Rescue Remedy (I have no idea if it works but I like the name) and read the *New Yorker* magazine because the cartoons make me laugh. Get me UNICEF on my iPhone, pronto. If they need to call me back, tell them I'll be power walking to Whole Foods. Join me. We'll burn some calories together. Then I'll treat you to some coconut water.

> *Do not walk behind me, for I may not lead. Do not walk ahead of me, for I may not follow. Do not walk beside me either. Just pretty much leave me the hell alone.*
>
> —Zen sarcasm found on Internet

Belief #3:
▶ CAST OFF YOUR WORLDLY POSSESSIONS AND YOU WILL FIND PEACE

If you think casting off your worldly possessions will help you find peace, dream on, sucker. Trust me, your karma (which is another way of describing the challenges you are stuck resolving in your life) will follow you regardless of location.

My friend went to India to pray on a mountaintop, and the first thing that happened was a bird shat on her head. When she finally got to the ashram they had run out of beds and she had to sleep on a cold, damp stone floor. The main guru there, taking pity on her situation, invited her to sleep in his bed. After three weeks, they began having sex, breaking his eighteen-year vow of celibacy. This caused utter havoc at the ashram, not to mention her expulsion. My friend had unresolved issues with men unable to make a commitment. India didn't solve them.

Bottom line, there is no way to escape life's dramas. I'm not saying that if your life is cluttered with junk you can't just clear it out and give yourself a more peaceful environment, or go for a long walk on the beach, or a vacation to the mountains, or move to Montana, if that is what floats your spiritual boat. What I'm saying is that there is no permanent vacation from life's crap. You can't drink it away, eat it away, screw it away, relocate it away, plastic surgery it away, Prozac it away, or vow of poverty it away.

Shoveling is part of your job. Using what you shovel to learn, adjust, and grow is also part of your job. Think of it this way: everyone on this planet is fully employed. Instead of the government taking social security and FICA from our wages, the universe subtracts a little pain, suffering, and duress each time you "get it."

My life is about "getting it." While I love consulting, writing, and producing my husband's movies, I am aware it is my B plan. My A plan is handling my inner ecology because it dictates the direction I take and the decisions I make.

I also suggest learning about Jatropha trees. They defy our cynicism. These miracle trees grow in tropical zones, are drought and pest resistent, have seeds loaded with biodiesel oils, and become potent and natural fertilizer after that. That's a lot of eco-bang for the buck. Of course, nobody's learned to domesticate them yet, but a little wild is a good thing. No one has quite managed to domesticate me either. I bet the same is true for you, you wild thing!

My karma ran over my dogma.

—Swami joke

Belief # 4:

▶ **MEASURE YOUR PERSONAL GROWTH BY HOW MUCH PEACE AND HAPPINESS YOU HAVE**

The metrics of measuring personal growth by how much peace or happiness you have will defeat you every time. Often, the more aware you are, the less good times you get to enjoy because the learning curve steepens. Have you ever made it through an entire day without something, even if it was relatively insignificant, disturbing your peace? Have you?

Before you answer, remember, you're not at peace if you are ticked off, irritated, gossiping, judging, blaming, hurt, angry or hating some circumstance or someone. Rather than evaluating how long the stretches of peace and happiness are in your life and beating yourself up because they're so short, why not focus on how quickly you retrieve them when the heavens unleash their fury?

When you suggest to your adolescent son he take his jacket to school because the weather has changed and he responds by telling you, "Stop mothering me and get a life!" are you able to quickly rebound from your dismay and:

- Stop yourself from whacking him with the aforementioned jacket and saying something you'd regret?
- Calmly let him know that response didn't work for you?
- Not take it personally, leave the room, happily going on with your day?

When your husband or wife announces over coffee he/she hates his/her life and only works to make money to take care of the family, how fast can you:

- Empathize without getting defensive?
- Listen without offering solutions because they just want to vent?
- Stop yourself from saying, "Fine, I'll get a damn job!" while slamming the coffee pot down in the sink and breaking it into six pieces?

When your New York taxi driver, en route to the airport, tells you he believes the Jews plotted 9/11 because he read that every Jew who worked in the World Trade Center didn't go in that day, do you have the ability to rocket back from outrage and:

- Firmly let him know that isn't your understanding of what happened?

- Tip him anyway because, although you loathe what he is saying, he still did a good job getting you to JFK?
- Imagine what his life must be like for him to believe something so wrong and hateful?

Evaluate yourself by the positive choices you make when circumstances test you. Applaud yourself on how fast you bounce back. Assess your progress on how disciplined you are at using your shovel to dig out from under the crud.

While you're at it, when you fly, consider giving an additional ten dollars to the airlines for carbon offset credits. There is a place at the bottom of every ticket that gives you that option. This will allow them to plant a tree for all the damage their jet fuel is doing to the environment.

Before God we are all equally wise and equally foolish!

—Albert Einstein

Belief # 5:

► **AN EYE FOR AN EYE AND A TOOTH FOR A TOOTH**

When you feel wronged, admit it, nothing feels sweeter than the thought of revenge. You hurt me, I'm going to hurt you, so there! If we allowed ourselves to indulge in acts of retribution, we'd be a civilization of blind, toothless creatures and optometrists and dentists would top Forbes Fortune 500 list.

Back in the biblical days, when that adage was written, the world was an even more literal place. Before there were laws, if my cow trampled your garden, you might kill my family. Or at least my cow. Now, that doesn't seem fair. In practice, a judge would not require you to come trample my garden, nor grant a garden for a garden exchange. Instead, I'd be required to replace what was lost (no "emotional damages" back then) with produce or duckets (cash, baby).

Still, the desire for revenge bubbles up inside us all the time. Unfortunately, or fortunately, depending on how you view it, those of us who are either less wounded or have the ability to resolve our wounds have a moral responsibility to behave in an even more compassionate way. Unfair? Sure. Does meeting crap with kindness and fairness, always work? Not always.

A close friend of mine had an experience that tested her commitment to peace. Her two beautiful dogs, both Scottish terriers, were viciously attacked by a neighbor's two canines. In the process of trying to save their lives, and before her neighbor heard the commotion and ran out, my friend was badly bitten, dragged on the ground, and seriously bruised. Her dogs did not fare much better and they all ended up in emergency rooms. It was a costly experience on all levels.

The next day, my friend went to see her neighbor to discuss keeping his dogs locked up and perhaps taking responsibility for medical bills. She had not reported the incident to the police, afraid they might take the dogs away and put them down. My friend is an avid dog lover, as am I. Her neighbor agreed to chain the dogs up and gave her his phone number in case there was another problem.

Two days later, a similar incident happened. Loose in their yard rather than tied up (as promised), the dogs jumped their fence and attacked my friend and her pooches. Back to the hospitals they all went.

Still hoping to resolve the situation without police intervention, my friend called her neighbor and was met, believe it or not, with a nasty response. He told her it was her fault for walking her dogs by his house and hung up on her.

The problem with the neighbor's suggestion was that my friend lives at the top of a canyon road and the only way out/down is to pass by his house. Dedicated to the values of her religion (in this case, Christianity), she tried another tack: a firm but still considerate letter insisting he contain his dogs and pay her medical bills.

After a week, when my friend received no response, she wrote again, and again a week later, but to no avail. Finally, she hired a lawyer and asked him to call her neighbor to resolve the situation. When that didn't work—her representative was told where to shovel it—her lawyer suggested she file a lawsuit, which she did. She also contacted animal control.

This was a painful decision for my friend (she's the sweetest person I know), not to mention expensive. When she commenced legal action, her neighbor went bananas. Expletives and similes were used that none of us were familiar with. At least we learned something.

This type of response went on for months—lawsuits are protracted, horrible, scary experiences. From the beginning, everyone she respected, with the exception of me, told her she was crazy for reaching out so many times with an olive branch. One lawyer she conversed with sent her an e-mail that said, "You're an idiot. When you're tired of giving peace a chance, let me know." Even though she was suing her neighbor, she prayed for this person daily. Sometimes we did it together, and sent "the light," a euphemism for good vibes.

Most of the time, my friend was able to successfully ward off her negative feelings but as it dragged on, she began to lose that control. Soon, her full-time job became managing her anger. It was like dealing with our carbon footprint. Still, she was tormented by feelings of wanting to destroy her neighbor and his dogs, and I wanted that result too. My astrological sign is Scorpio—you can mess with me but don't mess with my loved ones! We did every exercise in this book and finally calmed ourselves down.

The situation concluded when her neighbor's brother checked him into rehab for cocaine addiction, took the dogs to live with him (under strict guidelines from animal control), and agreed to pay the medical bills, but not my friend's legal expenses, which were now more than the emergency room visits. The only good thing that transpired was she had walked her talk, but that was a pretty big win. She stayed true to her principles, religion, and love of dogs. This allowed her to sleep at night, even if occasionally she dreamt of God turning her neighbor and his dogs away at the Pearly Gates.

Unfortunately, her neighbor probably sleeps at night too. People who participate in "wrongful actions" often have an acute psychological mechanism allowing them to justify what they do. That sucks the big one. You can only hope that one day they wake up to find the enormous amount of crap that needs to be dealt with and choose to pick up their shovel and get to work.

A pirate walked into a bar and the bartender said, "Hey, I haven't seen you in a while. What happened? You look terrible."

"What do you mean?" said the pirate. "I feel fine."

"What about the wooden leg? You didn't have that before."

"Well, we were in a battle and I got hit with a cannon ball, but I'm fine now."

"Well, okay, but what about that hook? What happened to your hand?"

"We were in another battle. I boarded a ship and got into a sword fight. My hand was cut off. I got fitted with a hook. I'm fine, really."

"What about that eye patch?"

"Oh, one day we were at sea and a flock of birds flew over. I looked up and one of them shit in my eye."

"You're kidding," said the bartender, "you couldn't lose an eye just from some bird shit."

"It was my first day with the hook."

—Anonymous story on the Internet

Belief #6:

▶ **NO PAIN, NO GAIN (I'VE REALLY GOT A STICK UP MY TUCKUS ABOUT THIS ONE)**

Human beings are masochistic, and the pain we proliferate makes planet earth a difficult place to live. No pain, no gain doesn't exist in the animal kingdom. Instinctively, animals avoid pain. Have you ever heard of a chimpanzee flinging himself from a tree and on to the ground to learn the inherent value of holding on to a branch? No. I didn't think so. Monkeys educate themselves by modeling positive behavior, thus bypassing unnecessary fractures.

How the heck did we get it so wrong? We're constantly repeating the same mistakes, doing things we know not to do, testing our boundaries to see what we can get away with, even though we know those boundaries keep us out of the minefield. Unlike animals, we have the capacity to learn non-experientially.

My mistake and what I learn from it can help you avoid a painful outcome. Your mistake can help me. But this gift is barely used. What a waste.

One of the reasons I got my master's degree in spiritual psychology was to study as much as I could about the human psyche. Like walking barefoot on broken glass, I wanted to side step as many excruciating experiences as possible. I'm not a masochist. I believe in evolution.

There is a psychological principle I invite you to integrate into your life nonexperientially. It has saved me from countless fights, heartaches, headaches, and losses. It can do the same for you.

The principle is: *the issue is not the issue, but rather how you are with the issue.* What this means is that it's never about the other person or situation. If you're disturbed about "something" or "someone," your upset is yours to track, investigate and bring to resolution. Resolution is not dependent on anything external altering in your life (the circumstances shifting or the person doing anything different) but rather on a change in your perspective.

Example: I have a new friend who is a name dropper. If I ask her how she is or what she's been up to, she answers by telling me what celebrity she's hung out with lately. It's always "this" party, or "that" get-together, or some restaurant story about meeting the "who's who" of the world.

Personally, I hate name dropping. I too have been around

people in the public eye my whole life, and they're crap shovelers, no happier than the rest of us. I even hung up on her once, while she was in midsentence! That left me with some shoveling to do.

I began to track my irritation with name dropping back in time and landed smack dab at my relationship with my mother, whom I loved and adored, except for the fact she was a major snob. With a voice like the actress Tallulah Bankhead (whose deep, raspy voice sounded like a man's), my mom was the first to tell you whom she knew and to frame that knowledge in a way that bolstered her ego. Her name dropping embarrassed me as a child and eventually I stopped having friends over to my house. I judged her fiercely and it was the source of great tension between us. When this name-dropping friend showed up in my life, it rekindled my confusion, hurt, and anger toward my mother.

With this awareness in hand, I did the only thing you can do to mend a past hurt. I went to the deepest place of loving inside myself and I forgave my mother for being a name dropper/snob and I forgave myself for judging her so harshly. I know my mom did the best she could to fight her enormous insecurities and I did the best I could at the time, given my age and consciousness, to deal with that.

Lo and behold, the next time my friend called to tell me what superstar she had just bumped into, I was totally fine hearing it. In fact, I actually started to enjoy her stories, no longer condemning them as inappropriate. In the words of Carl Jung, "Everything that irritates us about others can lead us to a better understanding of ourselves."

My pal, relationship expert Heide Banks, topped Jung when she sent me this quote: "God doesn't give you the people you want. He gives you the people you, need—to help you, to hurt you, to leave you, to love you, and to make you into the person you were meant to be." Ain't life grand?! Thank you, God!

It's never the things that happen to you that upset you; it's your view of them.

—Epictetus

Belief #7:

▶ **YOU CAN'T BREAK A PROMISE**

Actually, you can break a promise. While the backbone of your character is your word—it is how you build trust with yourself and others—life isn't stagnant. Life is always in flow and sometimes things change. There have been times I've committed to do something only to discover I really didn't want to do it, or could no longer do it. Perhaps I was just being nice when I agreed, or hadn't totally thought it through, or really believed in that moment that I was ready to participate.

In any event, you do have the right to change your mind. There is no shame in being a "flip-flopper." Like choosing what kind of car you want to buy, there is an eco-friendly way (Prius, MINI Cooper, Honda Insight) and a less eco-friendly way (a Hummer). Here are my three keys to ecologically undoing a commitment:

1. Honestly and unabashedly own the fact that you made a promise and are now going to cancel it. Do not lie by trying to convince the person you didn't really say yes. Do not expect the person to understand or forgive you. Simply stand in your truth, knowing you are not responsible for their feelings.

2. Don't judge yourself as a bad person for canceling an agreement even if it's important to that person or seems spiritually correct.

3. Here's the big enchilada: take the time to cancel the agreement inside yourself. Literally say out loud, and in the privacy of your home so your consciousness can hear you: "I am canceling my promise to do _____." Terminating an agreement with yourself is critical because your psyche withholds energy until a contract is complete.

To fully understand this, think of your brain as a computer. If you program something in and then change your mind, you must take the time to deprogram it or delete it. People with incomplete commitments are always tired. They are usually frazzled and irritable because they have broken the trust with themselves and that's a pisser. A broken pledge becomes a lie, and lying is toxic to your system and will eventually cause it to react or shut down.

This crap shoveler's conclusion: be one hundred percent accountable to yourself one hundred percent of the time. Practice a clean commitment protocol because accountability is a key to living a more earth-friendly life.

> *My husband has been producing copious amounts of green-house gases for years, but the temperature in the house has not changed.*
>
> —Wendy Flatus
> (admit it, crap shovelers, fart jokes are always funny)

Belief #8:
▶ **I CAN'T REWARD MYSELF UNTIL I'VE EARNED IT**

This is one of the most screwed up beliefs you could have. Some ungenerous, unforgiving, sadistic prick came up with it to torment us mere mortals. It has caused global deprivation for centuries, leaving good people starved for self-appreciation.

Until I was forty-four years old (I'm now fifty-three) I refused to reward myself until I had done something I deemed worthy. I wouldn't buy myself nice clothes unless I had closed a big deal, made a movie, or done something else of gargantuan proportion. Even then, I forced myself to buy only what was on sale, rather than getting the item I really wanted. I wouldn't dine at a nice restaurant unless I had reached a financial goal. Working my ass off didn't seem to count. Even when I made the bucks, I compromised and went to my third culinary choice because it was cheaper, and once there, didn't order the entree I pined for from the menu. I even denied myself the freedom to buy a scented candle to mask the smell in my bathroom unless I could justify it with some worldly accomplishment. My kindness to myself was directly tied to my professional wins. In the film business, and now in publishing, they are few and far between.

Thanks to some excellent therapeutic work, I am able to make what I call Self-Honoring Choices.

Self-Honoring Choices are:

- Decisions that exemplify generosity and caring for yourself and are not tied in to reaching a goal.
- Thoughtful ways you say, "I love me, just the way I am, imperfections and all."
- Random acts of self-kindness.

Some of my favorite ways of nurturing myself are:

- Buying flowers for no special occasion.
- Purchasing a bath item I won't use often that gives me immeasurable pleasure when I do.
- Getting a manicure even though I usually do my nails myself.
- Buying birthday cards without a birthday in sight (I'm addicted to the ones that play music).

Just recently, I realized I had slipped back in to a pattern of self-denial. I observed myself at the supermarket planning to buy flowers and cottage cheese, two items I like, but consistently failing to make the purchases. I pushed my cart to their respective aisles, put them in my basket, and then, by the time I reached the checkout stand, found some reason to leave them behind. I, of course, had the perfect excuse such as the expiration date on the cottage cheese was only one week away and I probably wouldn't be able to finish it by then. Or the flowers would be nice but I had meetings and dinners throughout the week and wouldn't be home to really enjoy them. I was stopping myself from having some simple pleasures in life because I didn't think I had earned them.

This behavior drives my husband crazy, absolutely crazy. He hates watching me do this to myself and I don't like it much either. So I took out my shovel and started to dig again. Guess what I had for lunch three days in a row? That's right, cottage cheese, as I gazed at my yellow roses.

You only have one life to live and every day is precious. More important, you are precious, even when you're stuck in the crapper. As adults, it is our "soul" responsibility, and no one else's, to nurture us. You are no longer dependent on external forces to provide love. You can be your own mother, father, and best friend, and if you had parents that behaved in lousy ways when you were a child, this is your golden opportunity to get it right. Life is hard. You deserve as much support as you can muster. Especially when it comes from within.

Our planet needs love too. Going green is a powerful way for you to say, "I care. I care about you, me, people I've never met all over the globe, people who aren't born yet, polar bears, catfish, spotted owls, meadows, marshes, and deep sea vents. I care about the giant swirling mass of plastic bits in the middle of the Pacific Ocean that are killing thousands of seabirds and marine mammals and fish every day because we can't remember to take some canvas bags with us to the grocery store. I care!"

The more you treat yourself with dignity, the more inclined you'll be to treat our planet with pride. People who don't know how to care for themselves are certainly not going to care about the environment.

No one can make you feel inferior without your consent.

—Eleanor Roosevelt

Bullshit belief # 9:

▶ **PEOPLE WHO PROCRASTINATE ARE LAZY**

If you're a procrastinator, or know someone who procrastinates, maybe this will help you understand procrastination and learn what you can do to alleviate it. The behavior of procrastination looks like this:

- You say you'll do something and then you don't do it.
- You make apologies and excuses for your behavior and promise to get the task handled, but you don't.
- Finally, under pressure, you complete your agreement.

This is an exhausting pattern for all participants.

Although many psychologists attribute procrastination to low self-esteem or unhealthy perfectionism, that is not my experience. I'm not saying that your self-esteem isn't battered every time you fail to complete stuff on time, but I don't believe that is the cause of procrastination.

When human beings want something badly enough they find a way to get it. They jump hurdles, climb mountains, endure agonies and never give up until the dream is theirs. If you're not going after what you want in a timely fashion, some part of your consciousness is in rebellion.

In my initial work with a client, I focus on helping them

clarify what they desire in their lives. Once we have that vision we create an action plan: things they can do to make their dreams their reality.

If the client agrees to certain responsibilities and consistently doesn't complete them, it's usually because some aspect of their psyche is not in agreement with the plan. That part is, nine times out of ten, a place called "the basic self." Think of the basic self as the kid living inside you who never grew up. It is the part that doesn't give a damn about work, goals, making money, making a difference, or shoveling the crap. The basic self only wants to play, dance, and have fun.

When you embark on a big new goal, it is essential to check in with your basic self and make sure it is in agreement with the hard work that lies ahead. Be prepared. The basic self will want to know, *what's in it for me?* If you don't have a good answer to that question, guess what will happen? You will procrastinate.

Over the last year I had the privilege of working with a talented young woman. At thirty, she was senior vice president of a major online marketing solutions company. Her core competencies were many and certainly included the ability to produce rapid results, thus leading to her early success.

Together we discovered her true calling in life: to combine her love of technology with her passion for education. She seemed committed to find a new job that would allow her to live her dream.

Every two weeks she would see me and each time, only two or three action items would be completed from our list that numbered at least twelve. Needless to say, this was unusual behavior for her and she felt very uncomfortable about it. She had no history of procrastination but procrastinating she was.

I observed the pattern for a while and finally suggested we do a technique to get in touch with her basic self. Through a dialoguing process, we discovered the aspect of her psychology that was totally freaked out about taking on a new job/life/mission.

The thought of more work wasn't cutting it. Without judging that place, or trying to bully it, which never works, we gently asked what her basic self would like in return for getting these things done. The "kid" inside my client told her she wanted to know, right then and there, that she'd get a holiday at Christmas and finally be able to have a good time.

With that information in hand, I tasked my client with deciding where she would like to go in December, even though it was only March, and told her to book the vacation immediately. She complied and within days was effortlessly completing her to-do list and has now embarked on her new career.

Was she lazy? No. Sometimes you just haven't taken the time to convince your basic self the path ahead is worth the time and effort.

I like work. It fascinates me. I sit and look at it for hours.

—Anonymous

Belief #10:

▶ **ONLY CERTAIN PEOPLE ARE BORN WITH THE INNOVATION GENE (like Einstein, Michelangelo, or the Google guys)**

Not even remotely true. There is a Steven Jobs, founder of Apple, inside of you! A study done by NASA proved that over ninety-eight percent of all young people are highly creative and that creativity, or the ability to innovate, is *unlearned* as you grow up.

Case study: 1600 five-year-old children were given a creativity test by NASA to determine which would be the most innovative engineers and scientists when they grew up. Ninety-eight percent of the five-year-olds scored as "highly creative." These same five-year-olds were retested at age ten. By then, only thirty percent tested as "highly innovative/creative." By age fifteen, only twelve percent. By age twenty-five, only two percent.

How sad is that?! Very. Which is why I travel the country busting this myth into smithereens by doing Innovation Workshops that remind people they are just as likely to come up with the next great idea as anyone else.

If innovation isn't a special gene, what is it and where does it come from? For starters, here's what it's not and what it is:

- Innovation is spontaneous. False
- Innovation is planned for. True

- Innovation is an event. False
- Innovation is a way of being, thinking, acting. True
- Innovation is creating something that has never existed before. False
- Innovation is the discovery of new ways of creating value out of ideas that already exist. True
- Innovation is the act of one great person. False
- Innovation is a team sport. True
- Innovation is comfortable. False
- Innovation accepts discomfort. True
- Innovation is instantaneous, a sudden "Aha!" False
- Innovation takes time. It is a focused process that comes out of relaxed, secure, and supportive environments that encourage thought and creativity. True
- Innovation occurs under pressure. False
- Innovation happens when you're having fun. True

The gap between what you can imagine and what you can accomplish has never been smaller. We are all innovators and the more we step boldly into those shoes the better off our world will be. Remember, innovation is the discovery of new ways of creating value out of ideas that already exist. Here are a few of my favorites:

An affordable machine that pulls water out of the air. The technology has been around forever, it's electrostatic (think of a dehumidifier with a filter), but now it comes in sizes big and small. For a three-hundred-dollar investment it can make gallons a day, which could save a lot of lives in the developing nations where clean water is lacking. As much as we worry about gas, water is the new oil of our lifetime.

Satellite radio took our love of radio, our ability to digitize information, and the existence of satellites to transmit signals and married them together. All three elements existed. What was "new" was the composition.

Who doesn't love **blogs**? They engage the art of editorial criticism and merge it with the capabilities of the Internet, giving everyone a voice like never before. The Huffington Post is my personal favorite.

In the banking world, **microfinance** is a major innovation. It takes the traditional structure of bank loans and makes money accessible to the very poor in a sustainable way. In the last studies I saw, over ninety-five percent of the poor people who take these loans pay them back. Those statistics drop dramatically when referencing the rich.

eBay just keeps giving and giving. It used the age-old system of person-to-person sales/auctions and created a global marketplace for the dispensation of goods and services. How brilliant is that?!

Wikipedia brought the encyclopedia into the twenty-first century by inviting the global community to create it. Wikipedia can be edited by anyone.

Reality shows morphed the art of documentary filmmaking

and our love of games/challenges/contests and made it a commercial venture. My good friend Ally would leave her high powered work as a laywer/venture capitalist/entrepreneur tomorrow, to be on *The Amazing Race*!

Maybe you will be the one to innovate how we learn, grow, and expand so we don't have to perpetually shovel the crap! I'm all for that.

> *When I do good, I feel good. When I do bad, I feel bad. That's my religion.*
>
> —Abraham Lincoln

Belief #11:
> **I HAVE TO SACRIFICE EVERYTHING FOR MY CHILDREN**

If you do decide to sacrifice everything for your children—your creativity, personal growth, individual spiritual advancement—then buyer, beware, you may also be sacrificing your kids eco-balance in the process. Carl Jung, the brilliant psychologist, said this about parenting and sacrifice: "Nothing has a stronger influence psychologically on the environment and especially on children than the unlived life of a parent."

Children are smart—very smart. Their caregivers are their gods and they want their deities to be happy. If you're happy, alive, and living life fully, your children will make their peace with almost all circumstances, including a little less of you sometimes—everything done, of course, with intelligence and balance. That balance must include your needs too. If you're happy, they're happy.

So here's the big bombshell: parenting is not creative self-expression. It doesn't fill that space. Parenting is amazing, important, fulfilling, and imaginative, but it does not address that part of your self that wants to express itself as a singular, creative being, making a meaningful contribution in the world. If more parents could embrace this reality, I think they'd take better care of themselves—be happier and less tense and their children would feel more secure.

Even though parenting is a big commitment, no argument there, it is essential to continue growing yourself, regardless of what it takes organizationally, emotionally or financially. Otherwise, a lot of negative things can start to happen. If any of these symptoms feel familiar, take out your shovel and get back to doing whatever you loved to do before you had your kids!

- You don't have the same amount of energy you used to have.
- You barely work out anymore because you just don't have time, right?!
- You find yourself wearing workout clothes all day long.

- Every day tasks feel burdensome and you are snappier than usual with your kids, spouse, friends, family—you get the picture.
- If you have a spouse or life partner, you only talk about the kids and that has become perfunctory and let's face it, pretty unstimulating.
- You stop putting on the perfume/cologne that used to make you feel sexy.
- You never shop for yourself; all your focus is on the kids.
- Date night, if you ever had one, is a fleeting memory.
- You feel frustrated with your life, even though you never tell anyone because you're an über-mom or dad or parental influence.
- You feel bored with yourself. You listen to yourself talk and it's really, really dreary, darling!

This is an erosion of your physical, mental, emotional, and spiritual self that you have allowed to happen. Catch the pattern and do something about it. Take a class, join a book club, get a life coach, find a way to individuate again. If you presently don't work, do a bit of the work you used to love from home. If you do work, and are keeping a job you hate for the money, then nourish your creative self-expression in other ways while you look for another job.

Don't wait until your kids are grown and out of the house to get on with your life. The way our economy is going your kids may never leave. Renew your sense of self now. The benefits are big: everyone in your family unit will feel better. You will also sleep more soundly, have more energy, be more authentically interested in your children's lives, make more time for your family and friends, find it easier to eat less (if weight is an issue) and look better because you'll be dressing nicer. Happy people exude a confidence that brings them results with less effort. Happy people also create a more peaceful world.

Found on a bumper sticker on a Hummer: *"Fe fi fo fum. I smell the oil of a hybrid scum."*

Belief #12:

▶ **I CAN'T HELP IT, I FEEL GUILTY**

Let's cut to the chase, because crap shovelers, you're almost at the end of this book. Feeling guilty is an utter, total, complete waste of time. Your time on this planet is not infinite, it's finite and you really can't afford to waste it, like we waste so many of our other natural resources.

Most guilt, albeit not all, masks a pattern of overresponsibility, which is what fuels the remorse train. Many people feel guilty because they experience an obligation, a compulsion, a need to help someone else take care of their crap and if they can't make that persons life better, they feel horrible about it. Unable to see the person suffer, they make it their job to "fix" whatever the challenging situations are, which either doesn't work or further disempowers their loved one because to feel better, the person needs to take charge of his/her life themselves.

I know about patterns of overresponsibility. I have suffered from them most of my life, first with my parents, where I became the adult child, and then with my husband—even though the last thing he wanted or needed was my help. He has never asked for my assistance and is appalled every time I tell him I think his well-being is my responsibility. This is called codependence, although people afflicted with it often call it love, and there are entire support groups to help people stop it. Luckily, right now, you have me.

Overresponsibility enjoys these exhausting characteristics:

- You feverishly work yourself to the bone to make life "great" for someone else, always looking for opportunities to help them. It's a mission you have been deployed to succeed at or die.
- You over give in every conceivable way, to the point of being utterly ridiculous.
- You are willing to do anything—even if it means compromising your own success—to help the other person succeed.

- You make decisions that compromise your own integrity but might "help" the other person (like asking a business contact to help them even if you had wanted to ask that person to help you, which would have been more appropriate).
- You believe you are a better person because you are willing to put the other person first—to place their needs ahead of your own—enter Joan of Arc . . . or John of Arc.
- You use any extra time you have thinking of next steps for them instead of solving your own challenges.
- You don't allow yourself to be happy if the other person isn't happy too.

Therapists successfully deal with patterns of over responsibility every fifty minutes of the working day. Therapy is the perfect place to heal irrational beliefs, people pleasing behavior and a sense of powerlessness that will weigh you down like a box of encyclopedias you're throwing out because the world has Wikipedia.

If you have to feel over responsible, then fixate on your relationship to our environment. Work like a mad person to "fix" the things you do that are not making the world a greener place. Too often, I dash out to the market, only to realize at the checkout line I have forgotten my recycled grocery bag at home. I have righted that by carrying a compact-size version in my handbag—no memory required (which is a great thing when you're in menopause, trust me). Take care of yourself so you can take care of others. Clean up your ecological mistakes and refine your eco-behavior. In my book, that's a winning strategy.

"Things don't seem any hotter than normal here in hell."

—Nick Abaddon, cartoonist

Belief #13:
▶ **I HAVE TO BE A NICE PERSON ALL THE TIME**

This kind of thinking falls into a category called "spiritual bypass." A spiritual bypass is a misuse of spiritual ideals, such as unconditional loving, acceptance, and forgiveness, to deny authentic feelings that come up around shoveling the crap.

Believing you have to be a nice person all the time to qualify as a spiritual being implies it's not okay to get angry. Well, it is okay to get angry. Your anger is not a "bad" thing. Your anger is real. Your anger is natural. Anger is part of life.

If you are someone, like I was, that feels enslaved by niceness, regardless of circumstance, you might examine whether your real fear is that you'll be judged or rejected if you let people see that part of you. You are most likely denying yourself the opportunity that anger brings forward to resolve unsupportive beliefs that have a hold on your life. Repression of any kind is out of balance. Repressing your anger, like I did, (until I went to one of the best anger workshops in the country thinking I was there to help a friend only to discover the depth of my rage) never makes the unpleasant feelings go away. All it does is make them lie in wait until the crap descends so dramatically no "good" person could possibly control themselves.

There are ecological ways to feel angry without adding to the emotional rubbish in the world. First, embrace your anger. Admit you feel angry. For at least a few moments, don't give a damn what anyone thinks about your anger—you have to start somewhere.

- Ask your closest friend if you can just "vent" from time to time. No advice necessary. Just a patient ear.
- Do free-form writing, which we discussed.
- Do more free-form writing!
- Treat yourself to a therapy session, even if you haven't seen your shrink in a while.
- Join a group where you can talk, share, and hear other people's stories. Empathy diminishes anger quickly.
- Do whatever gratitude techniques rock your boat. Gratitude lessens anger.
- Try a punching bag class at your gym.
- If you can't get to the gym, take a pillow and whack your bed for five minutes.

- If that doesn't work, try my personal favorite. Get in your car, roll up the windows, drive to an empty parking lot somewhere safe, and, at the top of your lungs, berate everyone and anyone who has pissed you off. Leave no survivors. If you are concerned about someone hearing you, blast your music while you rant.

Beware of using spiritual ideals to cover up your fear of picking up your shovel and shoveling. Ultimately, suppressing anger is a recipe for disaster and after what happened in New Orleans after Katrina, don't expect anyone will save you when a category four hurricane hits your life.

Anger management class closed for classroom repairs
—Sign on the Internet

Belief #14:
▶ **I'LL TRY!**

As Yoda said in the *Star War* series: "Try not. Do or do not. There is no try." Saying you'll try to do something is the beginning of the end. It opens the door to not getting what ever it is you said you'd do, done. The word *try* is a magnet for your incomplete actions, lame excuses, and failure to launch.

"I tried to work on my book, you know the one I'm passionate to write, but I just couldn't focus on it so I went to a movie instead."

"I tried to recycle more but I don't have room for those bins and I'm not sure about that water filter gizmo. Where do I buy it again?"

"I tried to finish my resume, because I hate my job and my boss is a primadonna, but instead I watched a rerun of *Dexter*." Talk about a guy with strong motivation.

In order to get your M.C.S. (Master's in Crap-Shoveling) you must delete the word *try* from your vocabulary. When you hear yourself say it, stop, take a breath, and rephrase. Instead of "I'll try to get the seating plan for the wedding done this weekend," consider, "I commit to get the seating plan done." Rather than "I'll try to finish the script tonight and call you tomorrow," how about, "It's my intention to finish the script." And when you proclaim, for the umpteenth time, "I'll try to change," consider, "I give my word to change," so everyone's life will be better. The language you choose is critical. Emotion follows thought. Saying what you mean will aid your success ratio. And I'm all for your success!

> *You can compete or cooperate, stuff or flow, withdraw or nurture, withhold or share, ignore or care. On the other side of your emotional needs is the essence of love.*
>
> —John-Roger

11

WHAT PEOPLE IN THE PUBLIC EYE HAVE TO SAY ABOUT CRAP, PEACE, AND HAPPINESS

*M*Y LIFE HAS BEEN blessed with an array of colorful experiences—from producing movies, to running film companies, to starting my own consulting company, to authoring books. It has given me the opportunity to interface with many well-known people. Now that I've resolved my issues with name dropping (hee, hee), I am honored to share their unique perspectives on life with you. The question I posed to each was the same:

When life deals you a challenging hand . . . when the proverbial crap hits the fan . . . what do you do or think that helps you get back to your peace and happiness?

This is what they had to say (Remember, human beings can learn nonexperientially!):

Deepak Chopra—best-selling author/spiritual guide (*The Seven Spiritual Laws of Success, The Happiness Prescription, Jesus: A Story of Enlightenment*):

> *For several decades I have embraced the wisdom of uncertainty. I wake up every day praying for even more uncertainty than I experienced the previous day. This allows me to be spontaneous and creative in the moment. I do not anticipate the future although, I intend it. As a result, I do not experience challenges; I look for opportunities. I am always conscious of being the seer in the midst of the scenery. The scenery comes and goes, but the seer is always there. It is the timeless factor in the midst of time-bound experience. I remain centered in the timeless and do not allow the time bound to distract me, although I enjoy it.*

Rosanna Arquette—actress/producer (*Desperately Seeking Susan, After Hours, Pulp Fiction, All We Are Saying, Searching for Debra Winger*):

> *When times get tough, I do my best to stay in the present . . . not to be so in the future. I breathe, which I do in my yoga practice, and it really does work. Staying present is a key, and being in the now. But don't be fooled, it's constant work and doesn't come easy. But peace and happiness are worth whatever it takes.*

Dan Shiro Burrier—Co-President, Chief Creative Officer—
OgilvyWest Advertising:

I often am asked, "How do you do it all, all those things you do?" The answer to this question lies in the question itself. Because if you stop holding the "things you do" as separate and distinct, but instead embrace them as your life, tension naturally dissolves. There is a problem in the words "this" and "that" which also create distinction— separation in Buddhist terms—and force one into the "juggling act." Again, the words matter. Juggling implies the management of distinct activities, separate from each other, which all have to be handled, caught, and tossed one at a time. Why are we spending so much time working to become master jugglers?

Consider instead creating a context that simply holds who you are, what you want to achieve with your life. A single context called "my life" that includes work and family, play and obligation, chores, sadnesses and joys into one unified whole. Then you get up and do it. Sleep when you need to. And move seamlessly along with this mystery called life. Within it. Not outside of it, trying to manage it.

No this and that. No need to balance this and that. No struggle between this and that. Just this. This. This. This. This life. And how do you start creating this context? Zazen.

Julia Ormond—actress/UN spokesperson (*The Curious Case of Benjamin Button, Legends of the Fall, Smilla's Sense of Snow*)— founder of the nonprofit ASSET, working to stop the devastation of human trafficking:

> *Sean Connery handed onto me this advice for when things feel out of control and out of whack: "How is your health? Are you eating well? Getting enough sleep? Drinking enough water? If not, get those things in place as your bedrock and you'll start to immediately feel better. If that doesn't resolve things then, you can start to process what's going wrong, but always start there."*
>
> *I know personally that if I have a meditation routine in place and a regular practice like yoga, everything else somehow follows, but you can leave it to me virtually every time I claim that I just can't find the time! As someone who has ADD, I find it enormously helpful to reevaluate my reality. I can get pathetically overwhelmed by six pieces of unopened mail—OPEN THE MAIL! Stress is very often aggravated for me by the unknown—it's often not six things to do, usually two, but while it's unopened and unknown it builds in my mind. LISTS—I make lists of everything I have to do, then go through and give it the deadline and go through it again and give it a generous and realistic time allocation—then I can see concretely exactly what I have in front of me, and it always gives me a better sense of calm. Then I need to call*

all of the people involved, confess I've taken too much on, I'm really sorry and here's my new realistic deadline. Once I've dealt with alleviating the pressure of someone else's expectation of me, I feel a bit better (and I know you're laughing at this Debbie, because I kept blowing my deadlines with you, and don't even know if this is gonna make it!). The icing on the cake to this one is to then align your to-do list and prioritize it to support your hopes, desires, goals for what you want your life to be. I never seem to get to this level, but can see the sense in it. A girlfriend once said to me that stress is about the unfinished things in ones life and that if you want to alleviate stress you need to finish all the things you started. And she called to say she'd done it and felt a thousand times better—she'd finished the ice cream in the freezer, the wine in the living room, all the gossip magazines she'd not gotten round to reading cover to cover and she felt great. Without being cynical I do believe that living in the present and clarity get blurred by the pull of stuff I've started to do or committed to and haven't finished, and the sad thing is that slows me down and dampens my energy. Just reorienting is my best strategy.

Peter Schlessel—President, Worldwide Affairs/Sony Pictures

Take a deep breath, realize that the win is not usually in the satisfaction of the momentary response and try to picture *how I would look through my daughters' eyes if they were sitting next to me.*

Catherine Hicks—Actress (*Seventh Heaven*)—Spokesperson for Catholic Relief Services:

I go to Mass. I dunk in water outside. I bask in the sun for ten minutes. I have a gourmet lunch at Gordon Ramsey's and wait in the window for my daughter to get home.

Carolyn Bivens—Commissioner, LPGA (Ladies Professional Golf Association, 2005–2009):

If my process of dealing with the big, controversial, public decisions helps even one person, that will be fulfilling. It might help to know that I was an Air Force brat. We moved frequently but never lived on base. This meant my family was the core of my support and socialization. Religion and discipline were central to my development and as the oldest of three, I received the full helping of Bible study, values, and manners. As unappreciative as I was through my teenage years and early twenties of my early lessons, not a day goes by now in which I am not grateful for the grounding my parents provided.

Next is the fact that women's sports have come a very long way (as the saying goes) but still have so far to go. There are challenges and boundaries which still confront women's sports organizations though the corporate world in this country has successfully broken through. So there are topics which are considered newsworthy in sports which wouldn't make it as an item in a company newsletter.

So there have been more than a few times the last three and a half years when life has challenged me to the max . . . when it hits the fan I go through a process.

The first thing I do is remind myself to keep my head. The more heated a topic gets, the more I work to maintain my perspective and patience. Next, I reach out to a constituency with knowledge of the topic but different opinions. The time for "group think" is not in the middle of dealing with a controversial topic but rather at the beginning to ensure we have included diverse points of view. Throughout the process I remind myself of two things: first, who I am is not defined by what others think . . . not always easy for a woman who grew up in the '50s and '60s. Second, my religion and the knowledge that God, my husband, and family is with me gives me peace and comfort before, during and after the challenges. And last but not least, I always try to learn from these sessions . . . I want to figure out what I have learned about either the business or the process or myself. After all, learning is like breathing . . . we do it or we die."

Sandra Bernhard—comedienne/actress (*The L Word, Roseanne, The Sandra Bernhard Experience, Sandra Bernhard: I'm Still Here . . . Damn It!*)

these are challenging times in which we live, i get up every morning, open the door and pick up the new york times and let out a gasp! where are we at? where did it all go so wrong? and how am i going to keep on the higher ground and enjoy my life? when i became a mother over ten years ago all bets were off, self indulgence, pettiness, selfish behavior had to be constantly examined and often put on the back burner. all the years of being on my own coming and going as i pleased shifted and curtailed. i used to be the kind of person who lashed out in bursts of anger when things didn't go my way, i would find someone to blame and dig in my heels, but when i saw my daughter display endless amounts of patience and wisdom i knew it was time to look inward and face myself in ways i had never done in the past. there is a real freedom in being able to let go of blame. i started to shift my needs and desires on all fronts, how much fame does one need, and what does it really mean day to day? i could see the beauty in my art, connecting to my audience night to night, running into people in airports who said hello and gave it up to me, i watched time flying by and what fame success and money began to mean and it just didn't hold up to why i became a performer in the first place. this is the big picture, but it all falls together the personal and public experience, because who i am day to day feeds the person i am when i walk on stage, it all becomes one, and since I never want to run out of the inspiration that informs my work, i realize that *i have to find real happiness day to day. to be able to step back and be meditative and call on the inner resources when things may not be just how i like them to be has really become the key to my evolution. to be, to tell the truth about what i see along the way, to never phone in my emotions with anyone to call myself out on my own shortcomings to keep complaints to a minimum all contribute to embracing my life and the ever changing world around me. above all to seek beauty and cultivate it in every aspect of life. this is what keeps me together, and enables me to reflect it through my work."*

Kelly Meyer—Passionate environmentalist/co-founder of the Women's Cancer Research Fund/heads the Leadership Council for the Natural Resources Defense Council (NRDC)/partner in the building of the first LEED Platinum home in California:

For deep cleansing and inspiration . . . I move. I go outside and move. I surf, I stand up, paddle, I run or hike and then things all seem a little clearer. The confusion, the roadblocks seem to fall away and the path to effectiveness and efficiency seems to appear. Exercising not only clears your mind but has a valuable by product of good health. It also connects you to nature that is essential in connecting us to the issues we face on the planet. We are all individual mini earths— we need, as Goethe says, to be the change in our selves that we want to see for the planet.

So as a coping method for "too much crap," Be green. Reduce the amount of stuff you buy, consume, and save. Reuse and recycle the "stuff" you already have by giving it to someone else that needs it more. And most importantly Rethink how you want the world to be. That vision will help you shift the choices you make every day."

ECO-TIPS:

First off . . . in times of economic turmoil we are reminded of our grandparents' generation during the depression. They were true conservationists due to their circumstances. All the little things that made us crazy about our grandparents are the ultimate green choices. Reusing aluminum foil, not throwing everything away to be replaced immediately with the same thing, turning out the lights, not letting the water run mindlessly, not putting more food on your plate then you can really eat, and thinking consciously about what is really necessary—these are all modern day "green" tips. The less stuff you have, the less stuff you buy, the less stuff you have to maintain and shovel.

Be free. Be green.

Reusable ecobottles on the go—get a water filtration system and drink from glasses at home.

Leave reusable garment bags with your cleaners so you are not throwing away all that plastic.

Take reusable grocery bags and produce bags for shopping.

Turn off the air-conditioning—open a window.

Turn down the heat and put on a sweater.

Use common sense. We all get it by now.

Daniel Powter—musician/composer—"Bad Day"—best-selling digital single of all time in the United States:

> *There are a few things that I do when life throws me a curve ball. I like to hike as it grounds me and fills my head with perspective. I also like to write out a list of ten things that I am grateful for. Finally, by being of service to someone else immediately makes me forget about my own problems. These are pretty simple things to do but they really help me keep my head above water.*

Dottie Herman—President and CEO/Prudential Douglas Elliman—has been named one of the "100 Most Influential Women in New York":

> *Throughout my life I have been faced with a number of challenges both personally and professionally. I have found that it is the challenges in life that make us stronger as they present an opportunity for growth and success. I believe you shouldn't feel like a victim during these times, and it is always best to*

stay focused on moving forward toward an ultimate victory. From every trying experience, comes a valuable lesson. I always try to stay positive, learn something new, and walk away from the challenge empowered and wiser.

Heide Banks—Author/On-air relationship expert (*Tyra Banks Show, Montel, Oprah*, MSNBC, Fox), National Spokesperson for Get Over It Day:

I try and find the humor in whatever challenge I am facing, figuring if its going to be funny tomorrow, and it usually is, then I might as well take the laugh when it is most needed . . . today. When that doesn't work, I turn on Lifetime TV to the most victimy movie I can find. I then recast myself as the star (with thinner thighs, of course), vowing that once the film ends so does my belief that I have no options other than being stuck.

Krista Vernoff—Executive Producer (*Grey's Anatomy*):

1. *Take a deliberate and intentional audible breath—it releases anything that's built up.*
2. *At the end of each day, while laying in bed, I think about three things I'm especially grateful for. When the crap hits—I try to recall some of those thoughts. Earlier today I recalled my gratitude for how entirely happy my son is . . . that pure joy only a thirteen-month-old can show. Like*

last night, he was running around the house just after his bath. He's refreshed, clean, and free—that pure delight on his face can take me out of anything I'm stuck in.

Billy Campbell—Actor (Ghost Town, Rocketeer, The O.C., Shark):

When the crap hits the fan I generally think of Epictetus— the old Roman guy—who suggested not worrying about things one can't control, and doing what can be done about everything else, then not worrying about that either.

Agapi Stassinopoulos–Speaker, author, blogger (Gods and Goddesses in Love, Conversations with the Goddesses, Huff Post):

I believe in tribes. I believe in finding your tribe—people that are connected to you and that you have a mutual caring for and where you have a safe place to tell it like it is. As a tribe, we are there for each other in every possible way. I have a tribe with my sister and Deb is part of it and other women friends that have earned the trust—and we lift each other, we project the best for each other and when the stuff hits we are there to comfort and care and laugh and know how each other 's patterns surface so the journey becomes sweet and graced filled. We must create our tribe and find its members or let them find us.

Jody Weiss—Founder and CEO—PeaceKeeper Causmetics, one of the top eco-friendly cosmetic lines in the world. PK makes donations to women's health advocacy issues and urgent human rights issues globally:

I have had my fill of challenges in my lifetime, from a physically and emotionally abusive childhood to an emotionally abusive marriage: a recreation of my early childhood home. And, these experiences have made me what I call a "wounded healer"; each one showing me where I lost "self" and "voice" in the situation . . . each one reminding me of what red flags I did not heed. Each one filled with more and more compassion for my self and the other person in the classroom called life.

For me, it is clear that there are two very powerful things that I can do when I am really in the deep of a difficult situation; both to transform the situation completely and revive me. They are to speak my truth in the moment (which I am still practicing) and to find some activity to bring me smack in the moment and not in the past or the future.

Speaking my truth . . . when I find that I am in a downward spiral with someone or I feel triggered by something they did, if I can say to them the way it made me feel, we can usually talk our way through it. I can usually do this with close friends very nicely. I still remain frozen like a deer in headlights with someone who is arrogant or aggressive, but

I am committed to finding the voice I need to speak up to even them. Speaking my truth self-actualizes my own value and creates more intimacy. It feels so good when I do it right.

The other thing I do when the world is just too much and I can barely sustain it is that I play with my dog Lucy (Lulu-Head, Smookie-Do, Dingle-Meister-of-Love) to bring me into the moment. The joy she brings me wipes away the issues for even a short time so that I can regroup, view the situation differently and recharge. I also do this through my art, which takes me into the most wonderful escape and when I technique, dance, and, of course, meditate. The weight of the world for me ALWAYS lives in the past or the future. I can always find my gratitude and abundance right here, right now.

Chef Akasha–Chef/restauranteur, *Akasha*, Culver City, California (private clients: Barbara Streisand, Michael Jackson, Billy Bob Thornton, E! Entertainment), author of *Hollywood Dish*:

When life gives me a kick, I love to get in the kitchen and make a great pot of soup or an Indian meal—curry, dal, rice, etc. Something about sauteing that brings me balance.

David Zippel—Tony Award–winning lyricist (*City of Angels*, *The Goodbye Girl*, *The Women in White*):

When I am down, there are two ways I usually cope. The first is to figure out a way to change the situation that is making me feel depressed. If I can figure out a path to a different result I can focus on changing whatever it is that is causing me to feel down. Having a plan or alternatives usually makes me feel better. The second is perspective. To realize that in the scheme of things, whatever is causing me to feel bad is usually not that serious and that even when it is serious, to look at how fortunate I am.

Penney Cox—Film producer (*Shrek, Honey I Shrunk the Kids, Terms of Endearment*):

I really believe in meditation. It seems so simple but what it does is carve out quiet time that allows calm and perspective to come back into play. And it gives me time to remember what is really important in my life; what is precious; the love of my husband and children; the joy of a warm breeze across the blue ocean; the smells of life around me. And third, I take my dog for a walk. I have a rescue and he is a walking bundle of unconditional love and endless forgiveness. Sharing all these moments of joy is what helps me return the joy into my life.

Arvin Brown—Theater/TV/film director (*The Closer, The Practice, Everwood, Hawthorne*):

The first thing I do is make sure that I've dealt sufficiently with any aspect of the challenge that lies in my control. Then, the issue becomes how to deal with what isn't in my control. To help me in whatever acceptance I have to find, I immerse myself in the aspects of my life that give me pleasure and ease. I travel because that's been a major excitement for me all my life. I read, making sure that I tackle something completely absorbing so that I'm not constantly distracted. And lastly, maybe most importantly, I reach out to the people who mean the most to me, if for nothing more than a solid evening of good food, good talk and embracing warmth.

Anna Getty—Holistic and Eco Lifestyle Expert/Director of PureStyle Living/Founder of Pregnancy Awareness Month/Eco-Editor, *Healing Lifestyles and Spa Magazine*:

In my life, I intend balance, peace, and inner joy on a daily basis. I do this by meditating daily, doing yoga, and hiking in nature a few days a week. In between I journal, check in with my ego, and read spiritually inspiring or uplifting books. Generally these practices keep me grounded during challenging times. There are of course times when things escalate and I react dramatically to outside situations and make them seem really big and challenging and then I try to up the ante with my practice and supplement it with a good therapy session, massages, acupuncture, or just getting away and resting for a few days in a spa or at a retreat or in nature. Something simple and grounding like taking off my shoes and walking barefoot in the grass, or like touching a tree or plant life. It's so simple but connects me to Mother Earth right away.

Dot Maver—President & CEO—Peace Partnership International:

Throughout my life there is one saying that I often share with others: "Change is the only constant." Knowing that we are spiritual beings on a human journey, and striving to live the unifying principles at the heart of philosophy and world religions is a steady focus in my life, as I adhere, to the best of my ability, to the wisdom of Gandhi when he said, "We must be the change we wish to see in the world." A spiritual practice of study, meditation and service is my foundation, and I consistently seek the opportunity in a given moment, seeking to identify and support what is emerging on behalf of the greater good without looking for results. My keynote is inspiring cooperation on behalf of the common good.

Lesli Linka Glatter—Film/TV Director (ER, Mad Men, Grey's Anatomy, The West Wing, Heroes, House):

When I was living in Japan, my mentor used the flow of a river as a metaphor for the ever changing quality of life and it has consistently brought me solace. Tsuji-san told me to remember that everything is always changing and that nothing stays the same so if things are absolutely terrible you know that it will change, it will not stay in the same place, on the other hand, if things are fantastic, that too, will change. It is the constant ebb and flow, and knowing this helps me not go to the depths of despair when things are rough nor be too attached when things are great. I also try to remind myself to enjoy the ride, whoever said 'the journey is the destination' has that right! I try to let go of the concept of "I will be happy when_____" (fill in the blank with whatever your list is . . . lose five pounds, make buckets of money, win an Academy Award, etc.) and be happy now . . . to be in the moment and see the joy all around."

Marta Benavides—spiritual leader and human rights activist/Nobel Prize Winner:

At this stage in my life, I can see situations with detachment. I can look at the situation and decide how I can transform it, to be more in alignment with my principles. I do take time to be 'out' of the situation by being in a garden, looking at nature, the sky, and if I need, I cry, or dance. But also I keep in mind that I can not ask for mangos from an orange tree!

Paula Mazur—Film/TV Producer (*Nim's Island, Vagina Monologues, Corrina, Corrina, The Search for Signs of Intelligent Life in the Universe*):

When crap hits my fan, I dig into what I call my Bag of Tricks. "Tricks" is a euphemism for measures I take to remedy the situation, ranging from autonomic activities like breathing to leaving the country. They are tactics, coping strategies. I have found them invaluable and happily share them with you.

1. *Breathe.* So simple. So hard to do. When under stress, our first impulse is to stop this most primary of activities that keeps us alive. Psychologists believe this knee-jerk reaction stems from our potty training days when we were trying to outwit our parents. Anthropologists believe it is a vestigial behavior from Neanderthal times when we were hiding in the bushes from large four-legged enemies and didn't want heavy breathing to give us away. Try inhaling six counts In, exhale seven counts Out. When your mind strays to your most tempting Worries, pull it back to In-Out, opting instead for almost instantaneous No Worries. Breathe until you can say: I am on this earth for a reason and now that I'm calmer, I'm going to remember what it is.

2. *Eat.* There's nothing like a good carbo binge to smooth you out. It is scientific fact that sugar substantially decreases anxiety and fear levels by rendering your brain unusable. I highly recommend several bowls of your favorite ice cream, or if you are lactose intolerant, danish is a great substitute. If you are lactose and wheat intolerant you could try a large bag of corn tortilla chips,

which with its high carbo count will be mind numbing and should be very satisfying, as food researchers report that "crunchy" is America's favorite food texture.

3. *Walk. Take a walk. It is ideal as it gives one the impression that one is not sitting in one's pile of crap but that one is making progress, moving forward, headed for greener pastures. Scientifically, the opposing arm—leg swings of walking have been documented to significantly reduce inner monologues of self-pity, fear, vitriol, and blame that tend to play endlessly in one's psyche when one feels like they are on the edge of an emotional precipice. Experts believe that if everyone took a nice, long walk when they got wound up, the homicide rate would drop by 73.2% and war would be no more.*

4. *Cry: Crying is so underrated. First of all, it is a proven wrinkle reducer. Second, it releases this amazing drug into your system that makes you feel life is actually worth living. Third, it gets it all out like nothing else on earth. Crying in public engenders feelings of compassion and empathy from people, which is exactly what you might need. If these people are responsible for your crying, it will make them feel guilty, which is excellent. If you are alone, don't worry. Merely lean your head to one side or the other and cry on your own shoulder. Follow this by patting yourself on the back and/or giving your self a hug. No, I'm not kidding. When was the last time you wrapped your arms around*

yourself and gave yourself a meaningful embrace? Maybe never. If you need help prompting a good cry, play your favorite sad song over and over on your stereo and let yourself come undone. Like a phoenix, you will rise from the ashes.

Annie Goeke—Eco-entrepreneur, activist, and educator/ Founder—Earth Rights Institute:

When the challenges are great and all seems against me, I commonly go to a place where I can do some inner reflections. Usually, I flee to a natural place—a beach, a park, a garden or a hike in the wilderness. It is there I console my soul and allow myself to release the burdens and worries that have been set upon me. And many times, I also do the ancient ritual of cleansing by burning sage with the intention of clearing the negative forces around me. But mostly, I tell myself that life is telling me- it is NOW—I need to go inward.

Robin Gurney—Senior Vice President, Imagine TV (*Friday Night Lights, Shark*):

I'd like to say that I take a deep breath, I meditate on my children and my husband, I think about Muskoka, Ontario, the most comforting and familiar place to me . . . and all of these things are true. But the thing that really helps me to find my way, that brings me balance and perspective, that gives me energy and peace . . . is a really good chat with a really good girlfriend. Louann Brizendine talks about how women need the communication of other women, that it is a hormonal and physiological need. It's true. An invigorating, questioning, amusing, and thoughtful conversation with a woman who I really trust is what I go to when I most need to retrieve my balance, peace, and happiness.

Christopher Gavigan—CEO/Executive Director—Healthy Child, Healthy World:

I stop and pray. Which for me, means I breathe and ask for help to calm down and it usually comes. But if things are really bad, I start to make a mental gratitude list. Thank you for my functioning limbs. Thank you for the pillow under my head and the roof over it . . . I start there and work my way up to thank you for all the love in my life.

Chad Rea—Founder—EcoPop—a social innovations collective that happily lives at the intersection of ecology and pop culture:

Every unique challenge requires a unique solution. Although companies and individuals seek my guidance, I am constantly drawing upon the wisdom of others to remind myself of the many lessons I also teach. I believe that the answers we seek are already within us. We simply fail to recognize them, especially in the face of adversity. When you start to value yourself as a teacher, you begin to deconstruct what is it you know, what you do exactly, and how you do it in order for others to easily understand and adopt. From there, it's really only a matter of learning to take your own advice when you need it most, which is a challenge in itself. In short, when life deals me a difficult challenge, I remind myself of what I know, what I would recommend to someone else, and then follow that advice.

12

WELCOME TO THE PARTY.
DON'T FORGET TO B.Y.O.S.
(BRING YOUR OWN SHOVEL)

*T*HEY SAY IT TAKES courage to see the face of God, because you have to see God's face in all people. The only way to do that is to move past your personality, prejudices, and points of view to the thread of oneness that connects us all. That means you have to see God, or the "good" (if you are not a spiritual or religious person), in all people, people you could justifiably have a right to hate. This includes, but is not limited to terrorists, sexual predators, CEO's who steal from their organizations, and all the hurt, hostile, angry human beings that negatively impact your life on a perpetual basis. If you are committed to compassion there are no exceptions to the rule. That's a hard nut to swallow, but swallow it you must.

To make matters worse, you're also asked, in the name of peace, to answer hate with love. Sometimes I just want to scream, "Gimme a crap-shoveling break! Get me Gandhi, King, Christ, or Buddha on line two!" The education, commitment, and practice it takes to meet hate with love makes becoming a Navy SEAL look easy.

But that's the journey we're on. Life is a classroom and each test is an opportunity to learn something. It is your responsibility to acquire the skills to overcome the negative and lead with the positive. I've had a blessed life compared to many, about which I am almost always grateful, but on the days I'm not, I am a snappy, sullen writer/consultant/film producer in a MINI Cooper. (Did you know that if every American drove a MINI we'd save sixty-one billion dollars in gas a year?!)

Finally, I've come to accept we are crap shovelers, here to shovel the crap, sometimes our own, sometimes other people's, because under the mess lies greater peace and happiness. Remember: manure is a powerful fertilizer. It adds primary nutrients to soil, binds the soil together, transports useful microbes, and acts as a conditioner. That's a lot of bang for the buck. Your M.C.S degree (Masters in Crap-Shoveling) functions in the same capacity. It will help you:

- Free yourself from judgment.
- Use your imagination for your upliftment.
- Discover the good in almost everything.
- Have a life plan.
- Know your greatness.
- Generate results that surprise you.
- Release your anger in a safe and noninvasive way.

These are organic strategies that work. They will help you recycle, reuse and reduce unhealthy mental, emotional, and spiritual emissions that pollute the world. Your gratitude, kindness, compassion, creativity, forgiveness, peace, and happiness are natural resources that won't run out unless you allow them to dwindle. Their social impact is vast. They create an internal climate change that has lasting and positive effects, despite America's refusal to sign the Kyoto accord.

Value your interior and exterior environment by buying fluorescent lightbulbs, recycling paper and trash, and driving fuel-efficient cars. Let's be eco-smart and create a greEnlightened society. Mostly, be nice to yourself and be nice to others and on the days that you fail at that, forgive yourself and do better the next time an opportunity comes your way.

In closing, here's a story that writer and spiritualist Eknath Easwaran told. I reflect on it often.

While we were living on the Blue Mountain in India, we noticed that our local bank had a very neighborly arrangement for collecting funds from the villagers. Poor villagers have very little to save, only a few copper pennies at most. To encourage them to deposit even these few pennies every day, the bank employed a boy with a bicycle to go into the village to their homes, collect their few coppers, and enter the total in their account. In meditation it is the same: when the Self comes, we can say, "We are no great saint, but a few times today we have tried to be patient. A few times today we have tried to put our family first. A few times today we have resisted some little craving for personal satisfaction." This is how most of us are going to make progress for a long time: a few pennies here, a few pennies there, collected every day. But in these innumerable little acts lies spiritual growth, which over a long period can transform every one of us into a loving person. To quote the bank advertisement, "It all adds up."

Life is filled with crap. Join the *Shovel It!* gang. You can make a difference!

In loving and peace,
Debbie Robins

P.S.: Please write me. I want to know how you're doing—the successes you've had using these seven crap-shoveling techniques and additional ways you've learned to turn life's crap into the peace and happiness you deserve.

deb@kickassadvice.com

RESOURCES
(SOME SHOVELS THAT HAVE HELPED ME ALONG THE WAY)

Here are thirty-two of my favorite books, CDs, educational opportunities, and nonprofits, as well as three transformational experiences I had while writing this book:

Books:

1. All books by Deepak Chopra, including his novels. I religiously read everything he writes, including his amazing blog, www.deepakchopra.com.

2. All books by Eckhardt Tolle. As much as I adored *The Power of Now*, I am enamored with his latest book, *A New Earth*. So was Oprah. We all know what impeccable taste she has.

3. *The Pathfinder* by Nicholas Lore changed my professional life! A must read.

4. *Family Secrets: The Path to Self-Acceptance and Reunion* by John Bradshaw—incredible information

about familial patterns. His genogram work (a template for a four-generational family tree) is the best out there.

5. *Momentum: Letting Love Lead* by John-Roger. This book reconnects me to the necessity to lead with my heart. It is always on my night table, just in case I fall, stumble, and hit the shut-off valve for my loving.

6. *I'm A Purple Cow* by Seth Godin—a small book that packs a sizable punch. It helped me define how I see myself. This is essential work if you seek to serve through public venues.

7. All books by Stephen Covey and his equally talented son, Sean Covey. If you hear they are speaking in your city or town, run to their workshops. Meeting Stephen Covey was a highlight in my life. The breadth of individuals and companies he has counseled is extraordinary.

8. David Sedaris's *When You Are Engulfed in Flames*. His writing is brilliant. We are lucky to have him around.

9. All poems by Rumi, particularly his poem inviting us to meet at a "place beyond right and wrong." I'm all for that!

10. All works by Eknath Easwaran—a sage, an avatar, a way-shower.

11. *Eat, Pray, Love* by Elizabeth Gilbert. In this fantastic book, I was awed by the author's willingness to share her authentic self with her readers. It strengthened my own resolve to be equally transparent in *Shovel It!*

12. *On Becoming Fearless . . . In Love, Work and Life* by Arianna Huffington, who I am proud to call my friend. Ari is a brilliant writer and, of course, an equally brilliant blogger. She is also the most fearless person I know. You will get your PhD in empowerment from reading this book.

13. *Of Love and Evil* by Hubert de La Bouïllerie

Educational Opportunities:

14. **ROCKPORT INSTITUTE**—a worldwide leader in helping people choose careers they love. Nicholas Lore, who coached me into my second career, has successfully transformed the professional lives of over 14,000 people. That's quite an accomplishment. Make sure he shows you the letter that President Bill Clinton sent him. *www.rockportinstitute.com*

15. **UNIVERSITY OF SANTA MONICA**, Los Angeles, California—Getting my master's degree in spiritual psychology at USM was singularly the greatest thing I've done for myself. It changed my life from the

inside out. I am forever indebted to Dr.'s Mary and Ron Hulnick, whom I believe are two of the most important leaders in psychology and transformational studies alive.

www.gousm.edu

16. **DR. JUDITH WILBURN'S ANGER WORKSHOP**—I thought I was going for the weekend to help a friend but I quickly discovered I was there for little ol' me. Having positioned myself as "the peacemaker" in my family dynamic, I had no idea how much hurt and anger I had about that choice. Being able to express my feelings in a safe environment—under the auspices of a brilliant psychologist—was transformational.

www.judithmilburn.com

CDs:

17. *Meditation of Understanding, Meditation of Forgiveness, Meditation of Objectivity, Meditation on Wealth* by John-Roger. There is an abundant array of meditation CD's available today. These are just my staples. I encourage you to find your own. Owning meditation CD's is a smart purchase. They are easy ways to enhance or retrieve your balance, peace, and happiness.

www.msia.org/store

18. Annie Lenox—*Sing* was my favorite song while writing this book. Remember, crap shovelers, "What doesn't kill you makes you strong!" Who luv's ya, Annie?!

Great organizations doing great work in the world:

19. **EARTH RIGHTS INSTITUTE:** Committed to securing a culture of peace and justice by establishing dynamic worldwide networks of persons of goodwill and special skill, promoting policies and programs that further democratic rights to common heritage resources, and building ecological communities.
     www.earthrights.net

20. **NATIONAL PEACE ACADEMY:** Mission statement: "Clearly what we are doing today is not working. We are exhausting all possibilities and yet we are still at war, have the highest incarceration rate in the world, the highest homicide rate in the developed world, and struggle with a culture of violence. We think the founding of a National Peace Academy will bring us a quantum leap closer to the society we all wish for."
     www.nationalpeaceacademy.us

21. **ASSET CAMPAIGN:** Founded by Julia Ormond and the United Nations Office on Drugs and Crimes, ASSET works to address the causes of slavery and trafficking at their source. Through its focus on supply chains, ASSET helps corporations, NGOs, and governments work to innovate and implement best practices for removing the economic impetus for slavery.
www.assetcampaign.org

22. **THE PEACE ALLIANCE:** Current focus is the campaign for a cabinet-level U.S. Department of Peace.
www.thepeacealliance.org

23. **HEALTHY CHILD:** A nonprofit inspiring parents to protect young children from harmful chemicals. HC is leading a movement that educates parents, supports protective policies, and engages communities to make responsible decisions, simple everyday choices, and well-informed lifestyle improvements to create healthy environments where children and families can flourish.
www.healthychild.org

24. **THE ALGALITA MARINE RESEARCH FOUNDATION:** Dedicated to the protection of the marine environment and its watersheds through research, education, and restoration.
www.algalita.org

25. **NATIONAL RESOURCE DEFENSE COUNCIL:** The nation's most effective environmental action group, combining the grassroots power of 1.2 million members and online activists with the courtroom clout and expertise of more than 350 lawyers, scientists, and other professionals.
www.nrdc.org

26. **ALLIANCE FOR A NEW HUMANITY:** Dedicated to connect people, who, through personal and social transformation, aim to build a just, peaceful, and sustainable world, reflecting the unity of all humanity.
www.anhglobal.org

27. **GLOBE AWARE:** Currently offers volunteer vacations in Peru, Costa Rica, Thailand, Cuba, Nepal, Brazil, Cambodia, Laos, Vietnam, Jamaica, Romania, Ghana, Mexico, and China. These short-term (one-week) adventures in service focus on cultural-awareness and sustainability, and are often compared to a "mini peace corps."
www.globeaware.org

A fabulous new resource I found for all writers/speakers/consultants:

28. **HELP A REPORTER:** this is Peter Shankman's gift to the world.

He helps match reporters/journalists with people like you and me, who believe we have something to say. How brilliant is that?!

Feel free to contact Peter at peter@shankman.com. *www.helpareporter.com*

An eco product I fell in love with:

29. **PEACE-KEEPER CAUSEMETICS:** I am enamored with this cosmetic line. First up, it is rated by the Environmental Working Group as one of the safest cosmetics brands in the marketplace. The lipstick colors, glosses, nail products, and lip balms, make me feel like a super model. Icing on the cake: PeaceKeeper gives donations to women's advocacy and urgent human rights issues globally, so while I am taking care of myself, I am also taking care of others. That rocks!

Transformational experiences I had while writing this book (because I'm a crap-shoveler too):

30. Heide Banks is a relationship expert and founder of The AQ Factor. She appears on talk shows and news venues, but really, in my experience of working with her, she is a truth teller. She has an uncanny ability to see where you are stuck and help release the blocks. Among many things, she identified my life long pattern of "rushing to get everything done so I could get it off my list" and showed me how to take my time and enjoy my process.

This brings me expanded freedom daily, not to mention an even higher quality of work. Thank you Heide!

heidebanks.com

31. Ronit Singer is a spiritual teacher who does energy work for personal transformation. I don't know how to verify the energy piece for you, but I can tell you that the transformational part is off the charts. By the time I sat down opposite her, she was seeing an aspect of my relationship with my mother holding me back from my greater success. As a result of our work together, I have experienced a rush of opportunity. No, a groundswell. Ronit has gifts. Big gifts.

    Ronit Singer: 212–614–3204

32. Now that I am living in New York City, Adam Sharon, L.Ac, MS, is my acupuncturist. He single-handedly alleviated the back pain I had for three years, in four sessions. He keeps my immune system strong which helps me avoid the crap of colds, flu's and other viruses. If you live in New York City, or are just passing through, treat yourself to his forty-five minute stress reduction session. He'll reboot your system and you'll be glad he did.

    adamsharonacupuncture.com, 646–943–4226

ABOUT THE AUTHOR

*D*EBBIE ROBINS IS A highly respected corporate, executive, career coach with deep roots in the entertainment industry. She is affiliated with the prestigious Rockport Institute of Career Change and Counseling in Washington, D.C., lauded by Bill Clinton as pioneers in the field, and the recipient of a Masters degree in Spiritual Psychology from the University of Santa Monica in Los Angeles, California. A world class professional, Debbie has extensive expertise in supporting clients in creating enormous success. Her vision and ability to facilitate growth is unparalleled.

For over twenty years Debbie was an established Hollywood film and television producer. She was President of Roland Joffe's Warner Brothers company, a producing partner with director John McTiernan and Donna Dubrow, a producing partner with director Penny Marshall, a Vice President at Disney and a producing partner with her husband, director/writer Hubert de La Bouïllerie. She produced *Calendar Girl*, *Amanda*, *Fat Man And Little Boy*, *The Right To Remain Silent*, *The Challenger*, *Samaritan: The Mitch Snyder Story*, and *Boner the Dog*, working with such talent as Paul Newman, Martin Sheen, Cicely Tyson, George Segal, Jason Priestley, Dennis Haysbert, Kieran Culkin, Laura San Giacomo, Amanda Plummer, Patrick Dempsey, Sandra Bernhard, Robert Loggia, LL. Cool J, and more. She has overseen the development and production of numerous other television and film projects.

Debbie's personal advice column, "Kick-Ass Advice", can be found on *The Huffington Post*, *Washington Times*, and *Donne Tempo* magazine. On the radio, she is the co-host of "Kick-Ass Advice for SBTV. Debbie is also the author of *Where Peace Lives*, which has been on two best seller lists, and enjoys endorsements from Deepak Chopra, Gore Vidal, Maria Shriver, Arianna Huffington, Penny Marshall, Jane Seymour, Debbie Ford and more.

Debbie graduated cum laude from Kenyon College. She and her husband reside in New York City and enjoy many strategic relationships in Europe. A tried and true crap shoveler, she shovels her Bernese Mountain dog's poop at least once a day. Visit her online at *www.debbierobins.com*.